Off the rails

The tale of two epic rail journeys

JAMIE MASH

Off the rails – the tale of two epic rail journeys

© Jamie Mash 2011

ISBN 978 1 4477 8911 6

Published by Mash Publishing

mashpublishing@hotmail.co.uk

All rights reserved. No part of this book may be reproduced in any form by any electronic or mechanical means, including information storage or retrieval systems, without permission in writing from the publisher.

First published in 2011

Also by Jamie Mash:

Invasion and deportation – a diary of Euro 2000 (ST Publishing, 2000), ISBN 0 9535920 4 9

Toulouse or not to lose – diary of an England football fan (Janus Publishing, 2000), ISBN 1 85756 402 2

Contents

Preface

Part One – East to West - Spring 2005

Introduction

Chapter 1 - Nova Scotia

Chapter 2 - Quebec

Chapter 3 - Ontario

Chapter 4 - Manitoba

Chapter 5 - Alberta

Chapter 6 - British Columbia

Chapter 7 - Homeward bound

Part Two – West to East – Autumn 2007

Introduction

Chapter 1 – British Columbia

Chapter 2 – Alberta

Chapter 3 – Ontario

Chapter 4 – New York

Chapter 5 – Massachusetts

Chapter 6 – Homeward bound

Preface

This book is the account of two train journeys across North America. The first, in 2005, travelling from east to west, from Halifax to Vancouver, and the second, in 2007, travelling from west to east, from Vancouver to Boston. I'd wanted to travel across North America, especially Canada, for many years, and the journeys described in this book have both fulfilled that ambition yet have also inspired me to go back for more in the future. The combination of the landscape, history and people, and the immense diversity within all of those, makes it all seem so fascinating.

The aim of this book is to convey the experience of undertaking such monumental journeys, describing the sights and sounds, thoughts and feelings, of two trips which marked the realisation of a long held ambition. By writing this book I hope to revive memories for those who have travelled to some of the places described, to give ideas to those who are planning a similar journey, but above all, I hope to inspire people to travel the world, to experience the world, and to realise ambitions. It's a big world out there and it's there to be enjoyed and experienced, and I hope that my written account of two journeys across Canada and north-eastern USA will inspire you to travel, particularly to the places I have visited on these two epic journeys.

Part One– From East to West – Spring 2005

Introduction

Canada. Just the word itself is an inspiration. It conjures up so many images, so many words. Take time to read these words, and think of the images they conjure up. Mountains, forests, glaciers, snow, lakes, plains, grizzly bears, polar bears, ice hockey, Mounties, the maple leaf, fishing, cold weather, warm weather, big cities, small towns. I guess what I'm trying to say is that Canada is such a vast country that once you get beyond the usual stereotypes, you realise that Canada is a country of such diversity, in terms of both its natural and human geography, although if any one image stands out above the rest, it's one of dramatic, stunning, mountainous scenery, with immense forests interspersed with lakes, an image of pure beauty and freedom.

Canada is the second largest country in the world, covering over six million square miles or 7% of the world's land mass. Its northernmost point is Cape Columbia, Nunavut, which is at 83°N, and its southernmost point is Middle Island, Ontario, at 41°N. From east to west, Canada covers six times zones, from Newfoundland Daylight Time in the east (GMT -3.5 hours) to Pacific Daylight Time in the west (GMT -8 hours). Its terrain varies from mountain to prairie, arctic to rainforest. Canada's motto is "From Sea to Sea", although this is geographically inaccurate as Canada has a third sea coast on the Arctic Ocean, giving it the longest coastline of any country in the world. However it can also be seen as a description of our journey, travelling from the Atlantic coast to the Pacific coast.

This book is intended to be an account of travelling across Canada rather than any kind of reference guide, so I'll cover its history very briefly. What is now known as Canada was inhabited by aboriginals from Siberia thousands of years ago, and then settled by mainly British and French Europeans from 1500, until Britain took control of all French colonies in North America after the Seven Years War (1756-1763). The remaining British North American colonies (after the American Revolution) stayed loyal to the Crown and were settled by Loyalist Americans and immigrants from the British Isles, and later by other Europeans. In 1867 British colonies in North America were united under the British North American Act to become the Dominion of Canada. This was initially the former colonies of Nova Scotia, New Brunswick, Ontario and Quebec, followed by Manitoba in 1870, British Columbia in 1871 and Prince Edward Island in 1873.

Since then Canada expanded to its current form with Newfoundland joining the country in 1949, with immigrants arriving from all over the world to give its major cities a more diverse demography. In 1999, a large part of the North West Territories became the province of Nunavut, and despite two referendums for independence in recent times (1980 and 1995), Quebec, which is largely made up of the former colony of New France, is still part of Canada. And we shouldn't forget the huge contribution made by Canada in both World Wars, and that the head of state is Her Majesty Queen Elizabeth II. And there, in a nutshell, and a small one at that, is the history of Canada!

The idea of a train trip across Canada really took hold about a year before going, in the spring of 2004. I'd wanted to travel across North America for years one way or another, but the extent of my journeys across the Atlantic hadn't got beyond a couple of visits to Florida and the Bahamas (both fantastic holidays). I first thought about a rail trip covering the whole of North America, which seemed very appealing given the availability of a North America rail pass for less than £300, which gives 30 days unlimited rail travel in the USA and Canada, but then I began looking at the train times and that journey would be 10 days solid on trains, and taking 5 weeks off work, staying in hotels and all the rest would be a touch expensive to say the least.

I then thought about trimming it down a bit, began thinking about the places I definitely wanted to go to and found that apart from New York, all were in Canada. Halifax because of its maritime and colonial history linked to Britain, and the thought that if I ever emigrated, Halifax would be a likely destination. Ottawa as it's the capital. Toronto as it's the biggest city, Niagara Falls nearby, CN Tower, and home of the Maple Leafs, my favourite National Hockey League ice hockey team (thanks to the NHL Playstation games). Jasper as it's high up in the Rockies, on the main rail route, and therefore ideal for using as a base to get a taste of the Canadian Rockies, home of surely the most stunning scenery in the world. And finally Vancouver, a large and diverse city surrounded by mountains and situated on the west coast of the second largest country in the world.

With a rail pass for Canada available for about £200 at the time, giving unlimited rail travel across Canada for any 12 days in a 30 day period, the trans-Canada option suddenly became the number one choice. This would cut down on train time and I reckoned on doing the trip in about 3 weeks, bearing in mind it's 3,900 miles by train from Halifax to Vancouver, and the trip non-stop (changing at Montreal and Toronto) would take about 5 days. As for the timing of the trip, I'd decided on the Spring of 2005 to give me the chance to save, the train tickets are cheaper (off peak until 31st May), and I wanted to see some NHL ice hockey, the regular season for which ends in early April. Looking at the fixture list for the Toronto Maple Leafs I found a couple of ideal fixtures, playing in Montreal on 31st March and the return match back in Toronto two days later, so I decided to base the trip on this.

I'd originally planned to go on 24th March, giving me time to see a bit of Nova Scotia and Quebec, but when I started researching flights I found that by waiting until 28th March, Easter Monday, I could get a flight from Heathrow to Halifax and back from Vancouver for £363, as opposed to the £505 I would have paid for going a few days earlier. It would mean less time in Halifax in order to get to Montreal and Toronto for the hockey, but the saving was worth it and it meant we'd have more time for the rest of the country. So with the special offer on the flights with Air Canada needing to be purchased by the end of September, it was time to see who was going out of those who had said they were up for it at some point or other since the idea first came to life.

Basic requirements for the trip were 3 weeks off work, a couple of grand and a credit card. At the end of the day there were just two of us who were 100%, so I booked the flights for myself and Chris, a friend from Northallerton, North Yorkshire, where I live. Anyone else who booked up later would lose out on the saving of nearly £150. So with the flights booked, which were non-refundable and non-transferable, the trip of a lifetime suddenly became a reality.

A few hours on the internet, several guide books and numerous discussions down the pub soon confirmed the route, encompassing one huge country, six cities, one small town, 3900 miles, over 97 hours on trains, and three weeks to do it all in. A couple of days in Halifax would kick off the trip, before heading over to Montreal and the chance to practice our French and cheer on their Toronto rivals in the hockey. Then the holiday's shortest train trip to Ottawa (hour and a half) to see experience the delights of the capital, followed by a few days in Toronto. This would be made up of ice hockey, the Niagara Falls, city sightseeing, and some nights out on the town, before heading out west.

We'd originally planned on going to Churchill on the south west corner of the Hudson Bay, to experience some small town near-arctic wilderness, but to go there by train would take 6 days out of the schedule and leave little time for the rest of the country. Winnipeg would be a good place to break the journey, being about halfway across Canada, and the break would certainly be welcome after a 32 hour train journey from Toronto, plus it would be good to see part of the country that we hear so little about, so we decided to stay there for a couple of nights. As it turned out when planning the route, the timing of the trains meant we'd have to spend 1 day or 5 days in Jasper, and given the schedule we'd be following to get that far, it was felt that it would be best to have the 5 days there. Jasper would be a complete chill out, a chance to experience the true majestic beauty of the Canadian Rockies, with walking, skiing and flying all options to consider. This left a couple of days to see Vancouver, with the optional extra of a day trip to Victoria on Vancouver Island before flying home.

As for travel experience, I'd been abroad a lot before Canada. Family holidays to the Canary Islands, Denmark and Norway. School trips to France, Germany and Switzerland. A lad's holiday in Rhodes. Numerous football trips with England to Holland, France, Sweden, Luxembourg, Poland, Belgium, Greece and Germany. And the two holidays in Florida and the Bahamas. But turning 30 makes you want to see more of the world (I was 32 at the time of going to Canada, Chris was 26), I wanted to see more than Europe, more than beaches, more than football. A rail trip across Canada gave me the chance to feel a real sense of adventure, seeing and experiencing new places, a new part of the world. My only previous experience of inter-railing was during the 1998 World Cup in France, when three of us bought inter-rail passes which covered France, Holland and Belgium, and we had a great time over there for 3 weeks despite coming home disappointed with the football as usual. We'd followed England around France, but also took time to make full use of the rail passes, seeing a bit more of Western Europe, and the fun of travelling around like that stuck with me. As for Chris, his only previous trip away from the UK was Amsterdam a year earlier, so he was also well up for the adventure of Canada.

By the New Year the flight tickets had been bought from Air Canada, and the inter-rail tickets had been bought from Via Rail, the Canadian rail company. These were bought direct from their website, to be collected from Halifax train station before the first journey at which point they would apply the charge to my credit card. The main condition of using the CanRail Pass is that you book reservations for each journey in advance, although this is at no extra cost. As we were happy with the planned route, we got the reservations booked up before going, but they could always be changed if need be.

The main drawback when planning the trip was hearing about the NHL 'lockout', which eventually led to the whole season being cancelled as the league and players union couldn't agree terms on their collective bargaining agreement. The whole concept seemed bizarre from someone who follows the game from afar, and with the NHL season cancelled that was the two Toronto Maple Leafs matches in Montreal and Toronto out of the window, but we decided to stick to the same train schedule.

When the season was in the balance I searched the internet for any lower league ice hockey we could watch to compensate, and discovered a team called the Manitoba Moose who play home games in Winnipeg, and were due to play their AHL match 3 hours after our 32 hour train journey from Toronto arrives there. The AHL is the American Hockey League, although there are a number of Canadian Teams competing, and it's basically the feeder league for the NHL, with each team being affiliated to an NHL team. So a visit to the Ticketmaster website in December secured two front row tickets for Manitoba Moose v Syracuse Crunch on 6th April. On the day of the NHL cancellation I also found out that the Hamilton

Bulldogs were at home to Grand Rapids Griffins on Sunday 3rd April. I didn't have a clue where Hamilton was until seeing it on a map on the AHL website, and found it to be in Ontario halfway between Toronto and Niagara Falls, with the game due to kick off at 4pm on the day we planned to visit the Niagara Falls. Perfect! So I bought another two tickets for that match, which meant we would be seeing two ice hockey matches in Canada after all! Who needs the NHL when you've got the Moose and the Bulldogs!

Looking into local travel in Ontario, it seemed a bit awkward to take in the Niagara Falls and Hamilton in one day, and would involve using alternative local transport or hiring a car, so the schedule was changed slightly by only having an afternoon in Ottawa, an extra night in Toronto, meaning that Niagara Falls and Hamilton could be done on different days using the rail pass. No problem in changing the reservations with VIA Rail, which I did by e-mail. So, at the end of March 2005, bags were packed, work was finished with for 4 weeks, and we were ready for the adventure to begin.

Chapter 1 - Nova Scotia

With us flying out on the Monday from Heathrow and England playing Northern Ireland in a World Cup qualifying match on the Saturday, it seemed like a good idea to start the holiday with a weekend in London, which is always good fun. Leaving Northallerton, North Yorkshire, my home in England's green and pleasant land, I had the same feeling of adventure that I had when leaving for the World Cup in France in 1998. Three weeks away from home, travelling across another country, this time in a different continent, this time across an entire continent, this time without 20,000 other Englishmen, just me and my mate Chris. For years I'd wanted to do a trip like this, for one year I'd planned this trip, and now we were on our way to, erm, London. Canada would have to wait until the weekend was over!

We stayed at my cousin Matt's house in Crouch End, north London, and had a good night out down the West End. England won the match 4-0, which we watched in the Maple Leaf Canadian Bar in Covent Garden. This was followed by a few more beers and then a superb Chinese meal in China Town, after which the three of us met Matt's mate Gerry and we ended up in a Dutch pub, which was full of Dutch people singing along to strange music including the Birdie Song! Good laugh though. Sunday was spent watching the boat race from Hammersmith Bridge, walking along the Thames (making various comments about the number of Australians in the area!), and having a few quiet beers.

Monday 28th March 2005

So finally, Monday 28th March 2005, 'Canada Day' had arrived! I woke up at 6am with not having had much sleep, and we were off down to get the tube to Heathrow (with a quick line of our version of the new number one hit 'is this the way to Amarillo', substituting Amarillo for Nova Scotia!). The flight left at 11-50am, slightly late, and I was disappointed to find that it was a smaller Boeing 767 which didn't have individual TV screens like I'd had on previous trans-Atlantic flights with American Airlines (Boeing 777) and British Airways (Boeing 747). It doesn't sound much, but I always like having the map in front of me showing where we are and at what altitude etc, as well as the dozen or so different TV stations. Still, having wanted to visit Canada for a few years, and having flown past it en route to Miami a couple of times, it felt great to finally be on the way there. With a book to read (one of the Sharpe books by Bernard Cornwell, as seen on TV starring Sean Bean) and classical music to listen to on the plane's radio, the flight to St John's soon passed and it was quite fascinating to see the ice flows around the coast. With St John's being right on the south east coast of Newfoundland, it was the first land we'd seen since flying over Ireland, and the cliffs looked quite dramatic.

After landing at St John's we had to go through customs and wait a few hours to get back on the same plane, collecting our luggage for it to be reloaded. No problems with customs, and the lady there became the first Canadian to hear about the big 3 week trans-Canadian rail trip! So with a couple of hours to kill what else could we do but go for some beers in the departure lounge bar?! First beer in Canada was Labatt Blue, which went down a treat. Thing was, no one was sure what the time was! Newfoundland, just to be different, is not just 3 or 4 hours behind GMT but 3 and a half. I knew about that beforehand but to make things more confusing, the UK had switched to British Summer Time the day before but Canada waited until the following Sunday, so we were actually 4 and a half hours behind UK time, which gave us an extra hour waiting to get back on the plane we'd just got off. Oh what fun we'd have with time zones over the next few weeks! So after a few beers and a chat with a Canadian couple from Chester, just outside Halifax, it was time to get back on the plane for the relatively short flight to Halifax.

The clear blue skies of Newfoundland soon gave way to dense cloud over Nova Scotia, taking away the enjoyment of the snow covered landscape. During the descent it was difficult to know what altitude we were at (no TV screen remember), although I could roughly fathom it out from what was going on with the plane. It was kind of surreal as we were going down, as I was listening to Blue Danube by Strauss on the radio, as featured in 2001: A Space Odyssey, which seemed to capture the moment perfectly. We broke cloud cover at around 1000 feet, landed and saw that it was raining heavily outside. No customs due to having gone through that at St John's, so after getting our bags it was time to head outside for a taxi. Halifax International Airport is about 25 miles outside the city, and after a short wait in the pouring rain we were on our way into town. It was a great feeling as we travelled along the dual carriageway towards Halifax through the forested landscape, finally in the country that I'd wanted to visit for so long, at the start of an epic journey, three weeks of what I like to call 'adventure'. The feeling of arriving in a far off land to see new sights and live new experiences is one of the greatest pleasures in life, and that sums up how I was feeling as we headed towards the city of Halifax, Nova Scotia's capital.

We soon arrived at our destination after driving through Dartmouth across the harbour into Halifax, the Waverley Hotel in Barrington Street which I'd booked before leaving via the Expedia website. Nice hotel, a well furnished Georgian style building, but very reasonable at just over £50 each for 2 nights for a twin room. Handy location too, in between the city centre and train station, which suited our needs. So after checking in and dumping our bags in the room, it was time to head off into town to explore. It was still pouring down, but fortunately my new £300 Aquascutum jacket was waterproof, didn't have a hood though so wore a hat to keep my head dry-ish. By now it was about 6pm (Atlantic Time), the shops were shut and the bars were dead. Took us a while to find any bars that were actually open, asked a couple of people and were told to head towards Argyle Street and Grafton Street, where we spotted a Cheers bar which was fortunately open so we headed in there for some refreshments after our long journey.

It was nice sitting at the bar, enjoying a few beers, looking out at rain swept Halifax, chatting to the nice helpful barmaid, thinking about the next three weeks of travel, with the normal stresses and monotony of life left far behind. I always enjoy the first drink at the start of a holiday, reflecting on the distance from home and whatever else springs to mind, leaving the trivial things in one's hometown far behind.

The barmaid, Rachel I think her name was, said it never got busy until after 10pm as they're open until 2-30am. Given our jet-lag, there's no way we'd make that time! After a bite to eat, very nice Cajun chicken sandwich, it was time to move on. Despite the temptation to stay, we just got the urge to see another bar. We went outside and it was raining even harder, so the Apple Barrel bar across the road was the next port of call. It was more of a diner though so just had the one beer in there, then wandered back down to Barrington Street and found a bar which was closed earlier, Gingers Granite Brewery.

It was quiet upstairs but nice and chilled out, and we sat by the bar again. The two lads behind the bar (Bucky and Brian) were a good laugh, so we sat and talked to them for a while, trying to get an idea of how Canadians think and what there's to do in Halifax. I asked one of them what Canadians think of Americans. After a pause, the reply, said with a grin, was "we tolerate them". This was followed up by a Canadian TV programme being on where they were taking the mick out of Americans and their heavy reliance on cars. Quite amusing.

They served their own home brewed version of Theakstons there, a beer originating in Masham, North Yorkshire. Chris tried and liked it but I stuck to my Labatt Blue. A band from Texas started playing instead of the John Lee Hooker they were playing previously, not bad, but it was still dead in there and with my body saying it was 2am after getting up at 6am after not much sleep, by 9pm AST it was time to crash out before I fell asleep at the bar. Nearly did in fact. Chris stayed on for a bit more so I went off on my own. It was still pouring down and the rain felt like it was being poured through a giant bucket of ice it was that cold! Certainly woke me up a bit. Back at the hotel I put some tunes on my MP3 player and then got some much needed sleep, content in the knowledge that the adventure had begun.

Tuesday 29th March 2005

After a solid night's sleep it was time to explore the delights of Halifax. It was still pouring down, but we couldn't let the rain stop us from seeing what had to be seen, so after breakfast at the hotel, a quick look on the internet in the hotel lobby when I booked a hotel for the Thursday night in Montreal via Expedia, it was time to head out into the rain, with Chris suffering from too much beer the night before. The plan was to walk along Barrington Street and then up to the Citadel via the Town Clock, then back down into the town. The Town Clock, which sits above George Street on the way up to the Citadel, looks strangely isolated, being of distinctly Georgian in design and bright white in colour, sitting on top of a rather non-descript shack type building, with just some drab sun starved grass for company, and the odd bit of rock hard snow. The tower itself does look quite impressive, having been built in 1803 and features a clock on each of the towers four faces, apparently so none of the garrison stationed there had the excuse of being late.

After taking a few quick pictures of the Clock Tower, trying to keep the persistent rain off the camera, we headed further up the steep slope towards the Citadel itself. Given the freezing, heavy and blustery rain, it felt like quite an achievement to reach the top of the hill, once we'd figured out where to go. The Citadel itself is a star shaped fortress completed in 1856, having been the fourth in a series of fortifications going back to 1749, when Halifax was founded by the British to counter the French fortifications at Louisbourg on Cape Breton Island, at the north east end of Nova Scotia. The constant updating of the fortification reflects the military importance of Halifax to the British at the time. Once up there we went through the archway, observed how desolate the place looked, saw a few workmen stood around, went to the main building, and found out that it was closed, for several more weeks apparently. Bugger! Oh well, no chance of seeing the museum and walking around the walls, but at least we'd accomplished one of our goals for the day, well two, the Town Clock and the Citadel, and what an achievement that felt! Okay, slight exaggeration, and we just wanted to go somewhere dry after that.

With it only being 10-30am and too early to start drinking on our one full day in Halifax, sitting in a pub all day was out of the question (although very tempting!). So after wandering around the quiet and rain drenched streets for 20 minutes, we finally found our way into the covered shopping centre (or mall as they say over there). It felt so good to get out of the rain! My body was dry and my head dry-ish, but my jeans got a good soaking, although they soon dried out in the warmth of the mall. It was actually quite nice wandering around that place, mainly full of very small specialist shops, not the big in your face shops in most malls that blast out poor quality music. I was determined to buy something other than food or drink in Halifax, and finally settled for a Swiss Army knife, just a small one which had a pen attachment and a dozen other things. It would prove to be useful for cutting off the tags of all the clothes I would later buy in Canada! At lunchtime the place came alive, with people coming out of the offices which are connected by the endless walkways in every direction. It seems that in Halifax you can go through winter without even going outside – drive out of the garage, park in the multi-storey car park, walk through a walkway or two to your office, another walkway to go for lunch, and same again to go back to work and back home. The concept of everything being inside or even underground is something we'd see a lot more of throughout Canada.

After a cup of coffee and a spot of people watching, which is always interesting when visiting somewhere new, we headed off in search of the Maritime Museum of the Atlantic, which is beyond the bottom end of George Street (which runs up the hill to the Clock Tower). We got as far as we could through the walkways, ended up in some office block and then realised we'd have to get soaked in the rain again. It was actually quite nice along the waterfront, and I imagine it's quite lively in the summer. We had a quick look in the indoor market along the way, which is a well presented indoor market (funnily enough) with a mixture of food stalls (loads of fish!) and various souvenir shops, but not tacky souvenirs in the least. One of them was full of interesting stuff, maps, books, flags, models, etc, but having to carry everything in a rucksack for three weeks across Canada prevented me from buying anything. The Maritime Museum itself was quite an interesting affair, with a history of the shipping around Nova Scotia in particular, and included exhibitions about the Titanic (it sank about 500 miles east of Halifax) and the Halifax Explosion of 1917, when two ships collided in Halifax harbour, one of which was carrying explosives and ammunition. The subsequent explosion killed 2000 people instantly and windows were broken in Truro, over 50 miles away. Nothing was left of the Mont Blanc, the munitions ship, and part of its anchor was found over 2 miles away. The explosion was also the biggest human caused explosion prior to the atomic era, and it's fascinating to read just how the event impacted upon the city for years to come. The museum and surrounding waterfront is definitely worth a visit and I hope to go back there one day, preferably when it's not as cold and wet.

Once we'd filled our head with knowledge of the sea, it was time to head back up the hill for refreshments, as it was now past lunchtime and we needed some beer! We went to Cheers where we'd started off the night before, and sat talking to the two barmaids Suzanne and Jenny. When asking what we could do they suggested going to the Alexander Keith's brewery where they do tours, so after a quick beer we headed down there. The mention of a free beer made the rain seem more bearable! Once down there we found that they only do the tours at weekends until the summer, so we settled down in the bar there for some of local brew, Alexander Keith's India Pale Ale. That beer was absolutely gorgeous. Luckily we found out that it was widely available right across the country, and to this day it remains my favourite beer by far. Unfortunately I've been unable to find anywhere that imports it to the UK, so I'll just have to wait for my next trip to Canada.

Anyway, after some much needed refreshments we headed back to the hotel for a bit, then back out to Gingers for a beer. As we were in Halifax, the biggest city of the Canadian Maritimes, it was decided that dinner just had to be seafood, so we went to the Five Fishermen restaurant just around the corner in Argyle Street. I have to say that the food there was delightful. They have a complimentary mussels and salad bar, so we got our money's worth there, then I had crab cakes followed by salmon. Lovely! Was a touch stuffed after that though, so struggled to drink much beer in Cheers (still very quiet) and Gingers (still quiet apart from some strange looking students), and as the jet lag was kicking in again, we headed back to the hotel to crash out. Before that though I just had to take a video clip on my phone of one of the things that had amused us in Halifax – a pedestrian crossing signal which instead of going "beep-beep-beep-beep" when it's time to cross goes "cuckoo, cuckoo, cuckoo"! It's mental. But then the crossing for the other road on the crossroads goes "cheep-cheep-cheep"! We were laughing for ages, the locals must have thought we were right nutters! So, after that little bit of entertainment, we went back to the hotel. And it was still raining.

Wednesday 30th March 2005

We woke up to find that for the first time since we arrived in Canada it wasn't raining. The train to Montreal wasn't due to leave until 1-05pm, but we had to collect our rail passes from the ticket office and we couldn't think of anything else to do, so we headed off down to the station after a late breakfast. The rain had gone but the biting cold wind was still there, although it was only a five minute walk the other way down Barrington Street to the train station. Halifax train station is quite a grand building and is very clean, but with only two or three trains a day it's also very quiet. We got our rail passes no problem, having quite a laugh with the bloke behind the counter who seemed to bit surprised that we'd picked the end of March to set off across Canada on a three week rail trip. The pass itself was accompanied by a reservation ticket for each of the journeys that we'd booked by e-mail. Once we'd got that sorted the two hours until train boarding time slowly passed by, with the help of my book, and as the station gradually filled up it looked as though there were about 40 people boarding the train, some booking their luggage in so that it would be taken on board and stored in the hold, some going 1st class with sleeping accommodation, others going coach class like me and Chris.

At 12:40 it was finally time to board the train, and after 2 hours sitting down and another 19 hours sitting down ahead of us, I was actually glad that our carriage was right at the other end of the platform. It was quite a moment to take in, walking alongside the grey steel train that was to start us off on our epic train journey across Canada. Once on board we got seats at the quieter end of the carriage (away from a couple of young kids who would no doubt be noisy later in the journey!), picking two seats each opposite each other. The trains run by VIA Rail for their long distance

15

journeys originate from the 1950s and were refurbished in the 1980's, but despite their slightly basic décor were actually very clean and comfortable, with plenty of leg room available. This particular service, from Halifax to Montreal, is known as 'The Ocean', and would take us north out of Nova Scotia, into New Brunswick, and then into Quebec following the St Lawrence river south west to Montreal.

So at five minutes past one, on Wednesday 30th March 2005, we started moving out of Halifax train station, as I said to the video clip on my phone I was recording - "here we are leaving Halifax at the start of a 3,900 miles journey". I'd end up taking about 50 such clips on my phone as a memento of the trip, although it wasn't until I got home that I realised that I could change the maximum recording time from 15 seconds to 4 minutes! One of the strange things that we noticed about Canadian train travel was the ticketing arrangements. Once they'd checked our tickets the conductor wrote 'MTL1' on a small card which he put on above my seat. This apparently meant 1 person for Montreal sat in this seat, which helps them find seats for other passengers who get on at one of the 26 other stops en route to Montreal, plus it lets them see whose tickets they've already seen, so it's actually quite practical on such a long distance journey.

For such a long train journey I had three essential books. One was the novel I was reading (with a second one as back up). The second was "The rough guide to Canada", which provided detailed information that would be sufficient for almost any visitor to Canada. Of particular use was the city guides, enabling us to get an idea of each city in terms of accommodation, nightlife and tourist attractions before getting there. The third book was the "Trans-Canada rail guide" by Melissa Graham, which gives a brief overview of the cities along the route of the trans-Canadian railway, provides useful information about taking the trip, and much of the book is made up of a useful detailed description of each journey, with points of interest highlighted. The railway in Canada is divided into sub-divisions of approximately 125 miles, and has a small marker every mile. This book makes a useful reference to this to describe the changes in the landscape and point out things to see. You might think that in a country as sparsely populated as Canada this wouldn't be very interesting, but it really does provide an essential reference source which helps you work out where you are.

The first few miles of the journey saw us pass through a very rocky canyon, and it took over half an hour of slowly rolling through the suburbs of Halifax before we picked up any sort of speed. It was nice to get a glimpse of Halifax outside the city centre, and despite the rain and our visit being restricted to small area, we left with a very positive impression of the city. The place has a very relaxed feel about, where people work hard to get on with their lives, but have plenty of time for each other and anyone else who visits the city. I think it also had a strangely homely feel to it, partly because of its history and partly because of that feeling that

England is just across the water, similar to Stavanger in Norway where one of my brothers lives, although there aren't any overnight ferries back home from Halifax as there was from Stavanger at the time!

As the city gave way to countryside, it was time for a late lunch consisting of a couple of bland rolls and a couple of cans of Labatt Blue from the buffet car. They made food on British trains seem appetising and value for money! The beer went down well though, and the food did the job. I made a mental note to visit the restaurant car when I next got hungry, either on that train or the next long journey. The scenery became a pleasant combination of pine forests, frozen lakes and wooden houses. It was time to use my other essential item for the journey, my MP3 player, which with over a thousand tracks on at the time gave me plenty of choice. Started off with some John Lee Hooker, a few random tracks, then got bored and talked to Chris about the football that night, England v Azerbaijan at Newcastle, a World Cup qualifying match. A mate back home, Chris, had gone to the game so I asked him to text me with updates.

After an hour and a half we stopped at Truro where a few more people got on, and then proceeded north. The scenery of northern Nova Scotia and then southern New Brunswick became very desolate looking, like tundra, which I suppose is to be expected given that the land was starting to waken up after several months of freezing snow cover, and much still remaining. There was a lot of flooding along the journey as well due to the snow melt, which added to the variety of the scenery. At 3pm Atlantic Time England were kicking off back home (at 8pm British Summer Time), so I listened to the National Anthem and various England songs, expecting to get a steady stream of text messages telling me of goals for England. This never quite happened, although my brother Dan sent me one saying England were losing 1-0, which was followed by one from Chris at the match saying we were one up! Had to believe Chris on this one, seeing as he was at the game and Dan would be winding me up knowing I would be sat on a train in rural Canada somewhere.

The train stopped at Moncton, New Brunswick, where quite a few more people got on. We still had a double seat each though, so plenty of room. Once past Moncton the scenery reverted back to forest, and there was a fair bit more snow on the ground. I'd also been without a phone signal for a while so had no idea of the England score. I noticed that there were a few French speakers on the train (a third of New Brunswick's population is French speaking and it's officially bi-lingual), and I was quite impressed at the bi-lingual ability of some of the passengers, with it being difficult to tell which language was their primary one. As darkness set in, I got a signal long enough to get a final score of 2-0 to England, not the expected goal feast but three points none the less. A few more people got on the train at various stops, we crossed over into Quebec sometime after 10pm (which meant the time went back an hour to Eastern Time), and by midnight I'd settled down comfortably on the double seat with the complimentary blanket and pillow that they give out for overnight passengers. It got a bit cold after a while so I ended up putting my coat on before drifting off to sleep, with the train making its way through the chilly countryside of Quebec. I awoke briefly at 4am, slept some more, then woke up around 7am with an hour to spare before hour arrival in Montreal. The weather outside was very sunny with clear blue skies, and the view across the St Lawrence river of downtown Montreal was very memorable, especially as we crossed over the river towards our destination. And so, 8am Eastern Standard Time, into the province of Quebec and another chapter in the great trans-Canadian experience.

Chapter Two – Quebec

Thursday 31st March 2005

As the train pulled up along the underground platform of the Gare Centrale (Central Station to those with no knowledge of French!), it felt weird to be finally leaving the train after 20 hours, but nonetheless a relief to escape the confines of a few train carriages. It hadn't been half as bad as expected, spending so long on a train, and was actually enjoyable in its own way, seeing the new and varied scenery with the ever-present sense of adventure. As we went up the escalators into the central hall of Montreal station, I have to say it's quite an impressive building. It's more like an airport than a train station, and with a stream of commuters rushing around clutching their early morning coffees, we were feeling like we'd just got off an overnight trans-Atlantic flight. The place is full of small snack shops and coffee shops, but noticeably French in style and very clean and modern. I had an idea of where to go to reach our hotel from looking at the map in the Rough Guide book (plenty of time for that over the last 20 hours!), so once we sussed out which exit to use and had got past the endless stream of coffee drinking commuters, we were out into the streets of Montreal.

The Novotel Hotel, which we'd booked into via Expedia when in Halifax, is on Rue de La Montagne, and should have been a quick walk up Rue Mansfield and then 5 streets along. The problem was, we went too far up Rue Mansfield and by the time we'd got to Rue de La Montagne, we were further up than we thought and past the hotel. So after walking the wrong way and then the right way, we finally found the hotel. Very smart, nice and clean, friendly receptionists, so after checking in it was time to get to the room and get sorted out. As tempting though it was to crash out for a few hours due to feeling 'train-lagged' (my new word for the energy-zapping effect of overnight long distance train journeys involving a change of time zones!), we only had one day to see Montreal, so after getting showered and changed it was time to go out and explore the capital of 'French Canada'.

We walked for about a mile down rue St Catherine, before turning right down another street to the next main road, the Boulevard Rene-Levesque, and back the way we came. Along here we found an entrance to Montreal's underground city, the vast network of pedestrian walkways spread out below the city. To put a number on it, there are nearly 20 miles of connecting areas, passageways and hubs beneath the downtown area, giving easy access to shops, offices and transport whilst avoiding the harsh Canadian winter. It was strange in that like the indoor mall in Halifax, much of it avoided the large over commercialised appearance of most shopping centres, and it was full of small specialised stores. Certain parts did open up into large multi-storey malls though, so with this it was time to start the hunt for some new clobber. It was here where we first found Canada's major two department stores, first Sears and then The Bay, which gets its name from the Hudson Bay Company.

The HBC was formed by Royal Charter in 1670 which granted the lands of the Hudson Bay watershed to "the Governor and Company of Adventurers of England trading into Hudson Bay." After the Confederation of Canada in 1867 and the subsequent Deed of Surrender in 1869, the Company's focus shifted as it concentrated on transforming trading posts into sale shops, stocked with a wider variety of goods than ever before. A modernisation program in 1912 and the acquisition of numerous Canadian department stores in the latter part of the 20th century made the HBC into what it is today, with The Bay stores being recognised as one of the major stores right across Canada. Anyway, there's the history of The Bay, where we both ended up buying more clothes on top of those bought in Sears.

Before travelling to Canada I'd found a very useful website which gave information on nearly everywhere in the world, this being Virtual Tourist.com (www.virtualtourist.com, funnily enough!). Being concerned at the reports of temperatures of -12'C in Winnipeg a couple of weeks before leaving, I posted a question on the Winnipeg forum about this and then one on the Toronto forum asking about nightlife recommendations, receiving useful replies to both. Among those to the Winnipeg question was from someone called Glenna who used to live in Winnipeg but now lives in Montreal. Anyway, to cut a long story short, as with many others who are registered on the VT website we arranged to meet up in Montreal. We were leaving a day too early to make another Montreal VT meet up, so it was good to hear that she'd meet us with some friends. I had no idea of her age or background other than a shared interest in travelling, but it was good to have someone to meet up with, especially with there just being the two of us. So once we'd finished our shopping I phoned Glenna and we arranged to meet up in bar called Publix, up on Boulevard St Laurent about 7pm. It looked easy enough to get to, just a walk of about a mile and half, down one street and up another.

With that sorted we had all afternoon to kill, without wanting to be particularly drunk before meeting Glenna and friends, and without having the energy for walking much further. In hindsight we maybe should have gone up to the Mont-Royal mountain for a view of the city, or even walked around the old town, but there's only so much you can do in a day so we settled for lunch in an underground mall. Seeing that the menu was in French I decided to order in French – "un sandwich au poulet et un café noir s'il vous plait" (chicken sandwich and black coffee please). "Would you like sugar with the coffee" was the reply. No point in making the effort to speak French then if they just answer in English! I thought my accent was quite good as well. Oh well. Nice lunch anyway. After that we decided to have a drink elsewhere and found a small bar adjacent to the IMAX cinema on rue St Catherine, so it was time for some Stella Artois and some people watching, seeing as we were getting a touch warm walking round in the sunny weather.

It was interesting sitting there, watching the world go by. Taking a break, sitting back and just people watching can be quite interesting sometimes, especially when abroad, and is a good way to get a feel for a place. It was early afternoon and many people were out on their lunch breaks, walking round in small groups with coffee in hand, smartly dressed, whereas others were more casually dressed. Overall the inhabitants of Montreal seem to be very fashion conscious, although some seem to be a bit over the top with what they wear. Basically they all looked very French, and there was a distinct difference between other Canadians or Americans. Have to say that there also seemed to be a lot of homeless people in Montreal which we noticed on our various walks around the place.

Not wanting to get drunk due to meeting Glenna later, I only had the two Stellas, Chris was not drinking, so we went back to the hotel to crash out for a couple of hours. We headed up towards Publix at about 5pm, with the intention of arriving early and having a couple of drinks before they arrived. After stopping to buy a new wallet on the way due to my old one literally falling apart, we finally found Publix but decided to have a drink in the bar opposite first. It was very quiet in there, and seemed to be more geared up for meals in the French café style, so we sat at the bar and ordered a couple of beers. The barmaids were good looking but very miserable and gave poor service. They seemed to resent the fact that our native tongue was English and not French, and a couple from Alabama sat next to us found the same. They were quite a good laugh, and were in Montreal to see some band who they were also going to see in Ottawa a few days later. They didn't have the accent that one expects from someone from Alabama though, the southern drawl, like in the film Forrest Gump. As for the bar staff, they took ages to serve us and were more bothered about eating their food than serving paying customers. One old bloke had a right go at them about the state of his pint of Guinness, turned out he was from the Basque region of France and certainly made his feelings known to the staff.

After a couple in there we went over to Publix. Much more lively in there and the first thing we noticed was how stunningly perfect all of the barmaids were, especially the maitre-d! Absolutely gorgeous! After about half an hour of admiring the bar staff, Glenna and her friends arrived. I'd send her a text message to say we were sat immediately to the left inside the door, and I'd also added a photo to my profile on the Virtual Tourist website, so she had no trouble finding me. Her two friends were Isabella and Phil, and all three were in their early to mid forties. The drinks and the conversation were soon flowing, but with the volume of the music it was a bit difficult to hear each other, so we went for a wonder further up Boulevard St Laurent to find a restaurant.

We walked for quite some time up what was quite a lively street, and finally settled on an Italian restaurant. We went in and sat looking at the menu but there was silence from all of us. No "oh, that looks nice" or "I like the sound of that". The menu was just so uninspiring and there was nothing on there that any of us fancied. So after a few looks were exchanged and a few short words, the question "shall we?" was answered with "yes, lets go" and we all got up and walked out. We hadn't ordered any drinks either, as the service was as bad as the menu. I'd never done that before, but the menu really was that uninspiring, not one thing on there I wanted, and the others all felt the same.

Glenna knew of a Portuguese restaurant a bit further down, so we settled on that. It was quite busy in there (surely a sign of a good restaurant) and we had to wait a few minutes before being seated, but we were soon seated towards the back of the restaurant, drinking red wine and looking at a far more appetising menu. We had an enjoyable couple of hours in there, talking about our various travelling experiences and drinking more red wine. Glenna lives in the outskirts of Montreal with her husband, and had an unfortunate skiing accent earlier in the year which had left her knee badly damaged, which meant she'd been off work for a while. Still seemed like a very positive person though who enjoys what life has to offer, and us all meeting up had definitely been worthwhile.

By the time we left the restaurant it was pouring down with rain, almost as bad as in Halifax, just not as cold. It was quite a contrast to the sunny weather of earlier. I was alright as I'd paid attention to the weather forecast rather than the afternoon sky and had my jacket with me, but Chris didn't bother with his and got soaked. We walked as far as Glenna's car parked near Publix, said our goodbyes then shared a taxi with Phil to our hotel, as he was passing that way. The hotel bar was very quiet, so the two of us just sat at the bar and had a drink, Chris then went up to the room but I stayed down and talked to the barmaid for a bit, called Marie-France. Nice girl, very French (should be with a name like that!), I told her of our trip and she said we should spend more time in Montreal. Fair point but on a three week trans-Canadian rail trip, certain sacrifices have to be made, and so the next day we'd be off to Ottawa for the afternoon before moving on to Toronto.

Friday 1st April 2005

I awoke with a slight hangover due to the mixing of beer, red wine and rum the night before, and we headed off to the station ready for our 10am train to Ottawa. We didn't bother with breakfast at the hotel, so got some food from the station before boarding the train. The journey to Ottawa was only scheduled to take 1 hour and 39 minutes, and marked the end of another chapter in the trans-Canadian experience, with our crossing into

Ontario after a fairly uneventful journey through the suburbs of Montreal and the flat countryside of Quebec. Our time in the province of Quebec was very brief, but enough to get a feel for the place. It's similar to elsewhere in Canada but with a distinctly French feel and identity to it, where they seem somewhat proud of their roots.

On the question of Quebec and separation from the rest of Canada, there's been two referenda in recent years (1980 and 1995) where they only just voted to remain part of Canada, so it may only be a matter of time before they do vote for independence. Personally I hope that Quebec remains a part of Canada. Within the confederation of Canada each province has it's own parliament and a fair degree of autonomy, and I fail to see what Quebec would gain from independence. Despite it's history of Anglo-French rivalry and warfare over the centuries, Quebec is an example of how the British and French can get along, where Canadians of both origins (and others) generally live happily side by side. And besides, Canada would look strange on the map without Quebec being part of it, with the Maritime Provinces being cut off from the rest of the country.

However, I don't really see the point in Canada as a whole having two official languages, meaning that signs and announcements everywhere have to be in both languages. Announcements in French in Nova Scotia just didn't seem appropriate. Why not make English alone the official language of Canada, with an emphasis on also learning French in schools? After all, Quebec became monolingual in the 1970's despite it's large Anglophone population, so let them keep French as their official language, encourage them to become bilingual so they can communicate effectively with the rest of Canada, North America and the world, and the rest of the provinces can have English as their sole official language. It would make more sense and be more practical, especially with English being the most widely spoken language in the world in terms of the number of countries in which it's spoken. English is recognised as the global language. And besides, who won the Seven Years War anyway?!

Chapter Three – Ontario

We arrived at Ottawa station just before midday, the journey taking a little longer than scheduled. The train itself was different to the long distance one from Halifax to Montreal ('The Ocean'), in that it was more of a British style train geared for shorter train journeys, with everyone having allocated seat numbers. The train station itself seems like it's in the middle of nowhere, and is about 3 miles from the city centre. After leaving our bags in the left luggage office for the afternoon, we went outside and got a taxi into town. Our plan was to see the Houses of Parliament, have lunch, wander around the surrounding area, and get back to the station for the 17:55 train to Toronto. The taxi driver wasn't the most communicative of people, and being of Middle-Eastern appearance it may be that his command of English wasn't too good. Still, we finally got him to understand "parliament buildings" and after a few minutes down the motorway and a few other anonymous looking roads, we found ourselves travelling up Metcalfe Street with the parliament buildings at the end of the road, getting dropped off just across the road from them.

The Canadian parliament buildings have a large open space in front of them and consist of three main buildings. The Centre Block, which slightly resembles the British Houses of Parliament with the Peace Tower in the centre which is comparable to Big Ben (or St Stephen's Tower to give it its correct name), contains the chambers of the House of Commons and the Senate. To the side are the East Block, which contains a number of restored offices open for tours, and the West Block which consists of private offices for Members of Parliament. After taking a few photos of the buildings we went inside for a tour, which is free of charge. I'd completely forgotten that I'd left my Swiss Army knife purchased from Halifax in my inside coat pocket, so had to hand it in when going through the airport style security checks. I was given a small ticket so I could claim it back afterwards, so no problem other than being a little embarrassed.

Once through security we had about fifteen minutes to wait before the start of the tour, which gave us time to read the historical information on display. There was about twenty of us on the tour, and our guide was the lovely Brittany, who asked where we were all from. I was quick to get in "England" before various other replies came in, Nova Scotia, Ireland, Toronto, Washington to name a few. The tour itself lasted for about an hour, and gave an interesting history and insight of the Canadian Houses of Parliament. It's similar to the UK, in that there's the elected lower house, the House of Commons, and the upper house, in this case the Senate rather than the House of Lords. And of course Her Majesty Queen Elizabeth II is the Head of State of Canada.

The Parliament Buildings were built between 1859 and 1866, after Queen Victoria had chosen Ottawa as the capital of the Province of Canada, formed after Upper Canada (now Ontario) and Lower Canada (now Quebec) merged. In 1867 Confederation was brought in and the buildings were immediately chosen as the seat of government for the newly created Dominion of Canada. The buildings were devastated by a fire in 1916 which started in the reading room and claimed seven lives, and after six years at the nearby Victoria Memorial Museum, parliament returned to the newly rebuilt Centre Block. The Peace Tower was finished in 1927. The building itself is very elegant and stately in design, with it's marble floors and subtle lighting, and there is a distinct sense of history and importance attached to the place. The parliament itself was not in session with the MPs and Senators being away on the Easter recess, so our tour was a little longer than it otherwise may have been. We had a glimpse of the Commons though glass windows, but were able to walk into the Senate chamber and have a look around from one end of it. It's remarkable just how similar it is to the British Houses of Parliament.

Once the tour was over and we'd had a quick look in the shop, then despite the option of going up the Peace Tower we decided it was time to head out off for lunch. In hindsight we should have gone up the tower, as it would have given a good view of the surrounding area and I always like to take the opportunity to do such things in newly visited cities, but I suppose it's an excuse to go back to Ottawa one day. For lunch we settled on the nearby Parliament pub, which is directly opposite parliament and across the road. The waitress in there was very nice, the décor was interesting with various framed caricatures of Canadian politicians all over the walls, the food was nice and the beer was most refreshing, our new favourite Alexander Keith's India Pale Ale.

After that it was time to go for a wander, so we went down Sparks Street Mall, which is just a long street with various shops and a few indoor malls in, and then back up Wellington Street which leads back past the Parliament Buildings. The large government buildings before the parliament looked very Bavarian in style, especially the roofs, and made an interesting contrast from the other architecture. Other than that, most buildings were high rise office blocks. As we were walking up there we suddenly recognised a couple walking towards us. It was the couple from Alabama who we'd been talking to the night before in Montreal, who were in Ottawa to see the same band again! Mental! We said hello and laughed at seeing each other and then carried on in our separate ways.

We carried on past parliament to Confederation Square, on the corner of Elgin and Wellington Streets, which is where the National War Memorial is. The memorial was designed to commemorate the "war to end all wars" but was not actually unveiled until 1939, months before the outbreak of the Second World War, and features 23 bronze figures representing people who fought in the First World War. The dates of the Second World War (1939-45) and Korean War (1950-53) were added in 1982.

After taking a few photos we headed back the way we came via a few shops. Tempting though it was to buy a totem pole in a native American crafts shop, we decided it would be a bit difficult to carry around for another 2 weeks, so I settled on a pocket book of native American wisdom. Not wanting to go too far due to the getting the train to Toronto later on, we were soon back where we started and decided to get taxi back to the station and wait around there. We had well over an hour to spare, and discovered that there was an earlier train to Toronto, so after amending our reservation tickets and collecting our rucksacks we got onto the 16:30 train to Toronto. No point in hanging around the station for an extra hour when we could get to Toronto earlier.

It's difficult to gain a solid impression of a city from just a few hours, especially when our visit was focused around one small area, but I guess our impression of Ottawa at the time was that it's full of bland office blocks and government buildings. That's a bit unfair really as I'm sure there's much more to it, and the Parliament Buildings and War Memorial were worth seeing. It would be good to have spent more time there, but as with Montreal sacrifices had to be made and we had a schedule to keep up with, so it was time for Toronto. At least we'd seen the essentials though.

The train to Toronto was scheduled to take just over four hours, but was delayed by a number of hold ups along the way and turned out to be a real drag. My book and my MP3 player kept me entertained, but due to feeling a bit tired and dodgy I just wanted to get to the hotel and crash out. We finally arrived just before 10pm, not long before our original train was due in, and headed out of Union Station towards our hotel, the Novotel on The Esplanade, which I'd booked via the internet when at the Novotel in Montreal. The thing that struck us upon arrival most was how tall all of the buildings were. It had a real big city feel to it, kind of like New York although I'd not been to New York at the time. I knew where the hotel was on the map and could see it from the train, but somehow we couldn't find it to start with until asking for directions. Once there we checked in only to be told that there were no non-smoking rooms available despite our request, so we had to take a smoking room and could change if it was a problem.

Saturday 2nd April 2005

Our plan for Toronto was to use it as a base until we left for Winnipeg the following Tuesday. We'd have Saturday seeing the city centre, shopping by day and drinking by night, Sunday would be Hamilton for the ice hockey, Monday would be Niagara Falls, before heading out west the next day. The weather forecast was predicting heavy snow for the weekend all over Ontario, particularly southern Ontario including Toronto, reversing the warming of the weather over the past few weeks. It would certainly make the CN Tower fun!

As it was, we found the room to be a problem due to the minging smell of cigarette smoke that lingered in the air. I gave up smoking 4 years previously and have become very sensitive to the smell and am a real whinger when it comes to smoking! Consequently waking up in the middle of the night to smell stale air conditioned smoke was no good, so in the morning we requested to be moved to a non-smoking room when available. After a very nice cooked breakfast consisting of sausage, bacon, eggs, beans, hash browns and tea, we headed out for the days adventure.

As predicted the snow had been coming down quite heavily, but with it being April it was that horrible wet snow that although thick, was a bit more like solid rain, unlike normal snow which isn't really a problem to be out in. As in Halifax though, the weather wouldn't be stopping us, and besides, most of what we wanted to see would be indoors. We walked along past Union Station towards the CN Tower. Daft though it was given the weather conditions, we still planned on going there that day due to having a plan to stick to. It's funny how difficult something so big can be to see, then suddenly you realise that it's right above you! The CN Tower is set back slightly from the main road, and you have to go through a couple of short walkways to get there. Once there though we were told that the tower was closed due to high winds and poor visibility. Can't believe we never thought of that one! So next on the list was the Eaton Centre, a huge shopping centre covering several floors and several blocks of downtown Toronto. Normally it would have been a pleasant ten minute walk to get to the nearest entrance, but given the wetness of the driving snow, we got a taxi up there.

One inside the Eaton Centre we soon dried out and set about buying some more clobber. We both ended up buying a Toronto Maple Leafs shirt, I went for the retro style white top and Chris went for the blue home shirt. We also bought more clothes in another shop, wandered around the place for a while before going for lunch in the huge food hall area. There's so much choice in those places, and it reminded me of the Sawgrass Mills Mall in Fort Lauderdale, Florida, where I'd been the year before. There was Chinese, Italian, Fish and Chips, Japanese, Burgers, KFC, Mexican, Sandwich bar, such a choice. We both went for a pizza and salad combination in the end. Very nice too. We walked around some more, looked at the more expensive shops on the higher floors, where a very persistent sales assistant complimented me on my Aquascutum jacket and said that Englishmen have such fine taste, and then decided to head back to the hotel.

By now the snow had turned to rain, Halifax style, so we decided to take the metro system back to the hotel. It was only about four stops back to Union Station which was the nearest to the hotel, so we then had a five minute walk through the pouring rain. Once back at the hotel we were informed that we had a non-smoking room available, so we changed rooms and then chilled out for the afternoon. We planned to go out in the evening, but had several hours to spare, so rather than sleep I decided to make use of the hotel's facilities. First off was the gym, just did half an hour but felt better for it. Not much equipment but full of TVs, which is okay for a hotel gym. The TV news was full of news about the pope dying. After that I went straight down to the pool for half an hour. As with all hotel pools it's bit small, and there was half a dozen others in and out of the pool, but it was good to have my first swim in ages. Once I'd got my healthy part of the day out of the way, it was soon time to be unhealthy and fill ourselves full of beer. After all, it was Saturday night and we were in the biggest city in Canada!

For starters we headed up Yonge Street and stopped off in an Irish pub called the Irish Embassy. The interesting thing was that on the outside of the building was a big gold plaque, inscribed on which were the words "British Colonial Building". How ironic! So inside the Irish Embassy in the aptly named British Colonial Building, we quickly downed four pints of Keith's to get us on our way. We were planning on getting something to eat, but after a few beers we both lost our hunger so weren't too bothered. We'd heard from some shop assistants earlier that most of the good bars were up on Adelaide Street and King Street, and a bar called 'Crocodile Rock' or 'Crocs' was particularly recommended, which apparently caters more for the late 20's and 30's crowd. Ideal for us then, so that's where we were heading.

It was still pouring down as we turned off Yonge Street and down Adelaide Street, and after what seemed ages without seeing a bar, we finally found one called Milwaukee and stopped in there for a few. Most people in there were in a large group, and we got talking to a few nice girls amongst them, one of whom called Ashleigh said that they were on a bar mystery tour of Toronto, and asked us if we wanted to join them if there was room. Sounded good, but when she checked with the lad who was organising it the bus was full, apparently. So after a few beers in there we set off again in search of Crocs, which turned out to be just across the road.

The place itself is a large pub with a couple of dance floors and a number of seating areas tucked away all over the place. It was fairly quiet to start with, but as things go when having a serious drinking session, all of a sudden the place is busy and a few hours have gone by! I seem to have spent most of the time in the corner talking to a nice young (well, similar age to me) lady called Meena, with whom I exchanged e-mail addresses and we briefly kept in touch after I'd gone home. Chris was busy strutting his stuff on the dance floor. After a few hours in there I got restless and fancied moving on, preferably to the place opposite our hotel before going to crash out. Chris was determined to stay in Crocs so I went off on my own in the end, getting a taxi from outside the pub to the Scotland Yard bar opposite the hotel.

By that stage I was a touch worse for wear, so can't remember much other than getting another rum and coke, standing near the bar, deciding I was too drunk to talk to anyone, before going back to the hotel and raiding the mini-bar in our room, which turned out to be a touch expensive to say the least! Chris came in an hour or two later, said he walked back after arguing with the taxi driver or something! Oh well, it'd been a good Saturday night, although we'd have an hour less to recover due to the switch to Daylight Saving Time overnight, Canada's equivalent of British Summer Time, which meant yet another change of our watches, this time an hour forward!

Sunday 3rd April 2005

We both woke up with steaming hangovers, and were still drunk from the night before, but with the train to Aldershot (to get to Hamilton) being at midday, we had to get up in time to go and see the CN Tower first, having missed out the previous day due to the weather. Talking of which, it was still raining! After a good solid cooked breakfast with lots of orange juice and tea, we walked through the rain to the tower. Still not ideal weather conditions but at least it was open and we couldn't go the next day due to going to Niagara Falls, so after a short wait we were on our way up the CN Tower. Once the glass fronted lift leaves the base of the tower it's on the outside of the building giving an ever more elevated view of Toronto. Although a smooth ride it takes your stomach a while to realise that it's left the ground, given the speed that the lift goes up, which I'm told is about 15 miles per hour or 20 feet per second. It reaches the observation deck, which is at about 1,100 feet, in just under a minute.

The tower itself was built between 1973 and 1976 by Canadian National Railway, and at 1,815 feet was the tallest freestanding structure in the world at the time. Unfortunately due to the high winds the outside observation deck was closed, and the precipitation at the altitude we were at was actually snow, but despite that the view all around was amazing. It was a weird feeling being so high up and looking down on all the tall buildings that we'd become used to looking up at. Despite the weather we could pick out a few landmarks, such as our hotel, the train station, the

Skydome baseball stadium, the Air Canada Centre (home of the Toronto Maple Leafs), and the Eaton Centre. Overall it's a fantastic view of the Greater Toronto Area, although on a clear day without cloud and snow it must really be amazing!

One of the things there that I was really looking forward to was walking on the glass floor. I'd walked on the glass floor on Blackpool Tower, but this is just a little bit higher! The looks of apprehension on some people's faces was quite amusing, but the floor consists of six types of glass of varying thickness and has the strength to hold 85,000lbs (38,556kg) or 14 hippos apparently (not that any hippos would fit in the lift!). It's still a strange sensation though walking over such a drop to solid ground, and it did get tempting to scare people by saying there's a limit to the number of people allowed on the glass at one time!

Once we'd satisfied our curiosity of the snow obscured view of Toronto and took plenty of photos, it was time to get to the station for the train to Aldershot. The lift down is just as good as going up, and it's amazing how quickly you're back at ground level. All in all an impressive experience despite the weather and a must see attraction on a visit to Toronto. After a quick walk through the rain we were soon sat on the train for the half hour journey to Aldershot. It seems strange that a city the size of Hamilton (population 490,000) doesn't have it's own train station, especially as the railway passes through the city, so we had to get the train to Aldershot station and catch a bus into Hamilton. The train to Aldershot made us realise just how huge the Greater Toronto Area and adjoining conurbations are, with there seemingly not be much open countryside on the way. Aldershot station is very small and basic, consisting of two platforms and some very drab buildings and concrete subways, but fortunately we only had about 15 minutes to wait before our bus arrived for the 20 minute journey into Hamilton.

Our only plan for Hamilton was to watch the ice hockey, the Hamilton Bulldogs v Grand Rapids Griffins in the American Hockey League, so other than that we just walked around the city centre slowly making our way towards the ice hockey arena, the Copps Coliseum. The city itself is rather large with a metropolitan area population of about half a million people, and although much of it's growth was based on heavy industry, it employs a growing number of people in the service industries. I've no idea what the suburbs are like but the city centre itself is quite attractive, with more of a small town feel to it. We went into a bar called the Blue Devil for some refreshments, where we were served by a very nice young waitress who we talked to about our travels. Unusually for me in a bar, I didn't have beer, or rum, or any alcohol, but instead went for tea and then decided to have some pasta for lunch.

The hockey was due to start at 5pm, so we had a very leisurely stroll through the shopping centre before arriving at the Copps Coliseum. We arrived over an hour before the game was due to start, so had to wait around for a while before going through the turnstiles. Couldn't believe it though when one of the staff there thought we were Australian! Good God! And I thought the Canadians were good at recognising accents! I suppose Hamilton doesn't get too many tourists though. The arena itself only had the lower tier of seating open, and although the official attendance was over 5,000 it certainly didn't look that many. The game was off to a great start though with a fight between two players after only two minutes. Great stuff! One for the video camera on my phone, although all you can hear on the clip is the little kid who was sat next to Chris shouting "fight, fight, fight, fight....." in school playground fashion.

We got talking to the two lads who were sat next to me, and they said they were from Falkirk in Scotland and followed Hearts at football and Fife Flyers at ice hockey. We had quite a good laugh with them, especially when one of the opposition players was sent into the penalty box, which was directly in front of us, and his reluctance to leave the ice prompted us to sing the British football chant of "sit down shut up, sit down shut up" (to the tune of the Big Ben chimes). It made a few Canadians around us laugh anyway. Other than our little outburst, the only song sung by the crowd, or more specifically one man near us for most of the game, was "Go Dogs Go, Go Dogs Go". That apparently is the main song that Canadian or American hockey fans sing, obviously substituting the name of their team. Alternatively there's "Let's go Devils" or whatever their team name is, I guess it depends how many syllables it has as to which chant they prefer. Not quite the inventiveness of British football fans but all good fun nevertheless.

One of the maddest things about the game was the in-game entertainment. At one point the players went off for a break and three people in strange looking "It's a knockout" style costumes had a race from one end of the rink to the other and back again! Then there were the people above tossing hot dogs (wrapped and sealed of course!) to the crowd. And then there was the playing of the "Good ole hockey game" with the words on the electronic scoreboard ("oh the good old hockey game, is the best game you can name, and the best game you can name, is the good ole hockey game...."). The game itself finished 4-1 to the Bulldogs so the crowd went home happy, but the players saved the best until last by having a massive brawl at the end of the game, involving practically every player and lasting for minutes! Great stuff!

Once outside we found that it was still raining, so we walked back through the shopping centre for most of the way. Once back at the bus station we had about 45 minutes to wait for the bus, and by now it was pretty cold. Back to Aldershot station and the place was practically deserted. The ticket office and kiosk were closing, and there was nothing there or on the platforms to indicate which platform we needed for the train back to Toronto. We had a good idea, assuming that it would be opposite the one we got off earlier, but with both sides of the station looking identical and the lack of people anywhere, that was a touch difficult. After nearly an hour in a shelter on a wet, dark, deserted station, other passengers finally turned up to confirm we were on the right side, and it was quite a relief when the train finally pulled in. We arrived back in Toronto just before 9-30pm, both knackered, so grabbed a sandwich at the station for dinner and went back to the hotel to crash out. I was quite proud of myself having had my first alcohol free day of the trip so far!

Monday 4th April 2005

Monday morning, a week of the trip gone and two weeks to go, and it was a bright sunny day. It would have been perfect for the CN Tower, but we had to catch the 09-40 train to Niagara Falls, which would get us there just before midday. The train that we were on went all the way to New York City, and was an Amtrak one rather than VIA Rail. It felt good to see the sun and clear blue skies, and as we passed out of Toronto alongside Lake Ontario, then past Hamilton, we began to get an idea of the view that could be enjoyed from the CN Tower on a clear day. Even as we approached Niagara Falls we could still see the tower above the horizon over the lake. As we neared the station there were various announcements about passport control checks for those staying on the train beyond Niagara Falls (Canada), but that was of no concern to us as were getting off on the Canadian side of the border. The station itself is very small, and once outside we had no idea which way it was to the falls, although we had a rough idea of the direction having not passed it on the train.

As I'd mentioned previously, there'd been a lot of snow forecast for the weekend in southern Ontario, and this place had over a foot of fresh snow fall over the weekend, which was mostly still there to reflect the bright sunlight, making it a touch difficult to see given that I'd left my sunglasses back at the hotel. Fortunately there was a taxi available to resolve our transport problem, so we took that down to the main viewing area, feeling the anticipation of seeing the falls for the first time as we got nearer. The taxi dropped us just outside the main visitor centre next to the Horseshoe Falls, and we went straight through there to get to the viewpoint. To our right and straight in front of us was the Horseshoe Falls, which funnily enough are in a kind of horseshoe shape, and are by far the bigger of the two falls. We were stood about 20 feet above the water, just before the drop, and the scale of the thing is amazing. Like many things that you see for the first time and have been looking forward to seeing, I found myself taking endless pictures and video clips before just stopping and taking in the wonder of what was in front of me.

Having said that, it's amazing how many different camera angles you can get of a huge waterfall, so I ended up taking quite a few pictures, once I'd managed to avoid sliding over on the ice covered ground! I sent a picture of the falls via SMS to a couple of friends at work, and after about half an hour there we walked up along the side of the river to get a better view of the American Falls, which are on the USA side of the border. Although impressive in their own right, they seem somewhat dwarfed by the Horseshoe Falls. It's a nice walk along there, and our plan was to walk over the Rainbow Bridge into the USA for a beer. When we reached the bridge we found that the pavement was covered in slushy snow which was a real pain to walk on, sliding around everywhere, but we stopped halfway where there is a plaque to mark the international boundary line between Canada and the USA. This prompted me to take a video clip of being "in Canada, in the US, in Canada, US, Canada, beer…" as I stepped from one side to the other. I'm easily amused!

Once at the American side of the bridge we had to go through US Customs, which to be honest seemed a little excessive for a land border with Canada. First we had to fill in the green card to waive the requirement for a visa, and then answer various questions about our visit. "How long do you intend to stay in the United States?" "About an hour." "What's the purpose of your visit?" "To have a beer and maybe some lunch, and have a look around". "Have you ever been arrested anywhere in the world?" At this point I became a little worried as I'd received a formal caution for a minor public order offence in York three years previously when out drinking, and as far as I knew they could have had it up on their computer after scanning my passport. "Erm, yes, just a minor public order offence…" "Pardon me?" "…but I wasn't charged for it". "That's okay then". "Phew", I thought. So after all those questions and after paying the $6 entry fee, we were in the United States of America. New York State in fact. Seems a bit steep to pay $6 just to walk into the USA, but it had to be done. We had no idea what was on the American side of the border, so just walked a few hundred yards until we found a bar, the Hard Rock Café.

It was fairly quiet in there but we stayed for a couple of beers and some lunch, after I'd sent a text to my cousin Dominique to say that I was having lunch in New York (state). As we walked around some almost deserted gift shops around the corner, the sun became so bright reflecting off the snow that I could hardly keep my eyes open, as the snow around there was relatively undisturbed. I almost bought some cheap plastic sunglasses for the day, but didn't bother in the end. Chris was totally unimpressed with America, having satisfied his curiosity by an hour's visit over the border, so with nothing else to do we walked back over the Canada. Just as were we halfway over the bridge, joking about the US and revoking their declaration of independence, a car goes past at speed through a deep puddle of melt water and totally soaks the pair of us! I couldn't believe it, felt like someone had just tipped a bucket of cold water over me! Nothing that could be done though, they weren't stopping so after shouting a few profanities we kind of laughed about it and joked with some other people coming in the opposite direction. Even got a hint of a smile from the Canadian customs official, especially when Chris said he's never going back to America ever again.

Fortunately it was just snow melt water from the bridge, and not full of crap from drains and buildings, so it was fairly clean and we didn't stink of anything, and we soon dried out with the aid of some paper towels in a nearby toilet. Had to laugh in the toilet we went to though. When I walked in to get some paper towels to dry myself with I noticed a figure stood in the corner at the urinal, thought nothing of it until I looked again and saw it was a man sized stuffed figure with a moose's head stood there, dressed in jeans and a checked shirt! It looked mental! After a quick look around the gift shop in which I bought a load of postcards to send home (well, not to my home, but you know what I mean!), we walked up the street away from the falls area, with no particular aim of where to go. I have to say though I've never seen as much tack in one place, it makes Blackpool seafront look classy! The whole street is shop after shop of tacky seaside type toys and amusements. All we wanted was a bar but it took a while to find one amongst all that tack, finally finding a TGI Fridays bar down the road. I took the opportunity to write my postcards whilst having a couple of beers, and got talking to the bar staff about our trip, one of whom is from Winnipeg and gave us a few tips on places to go.

We decided to walk back to the train station seeing as we had plenty of time to spare before the 17-45 train back to Toronto. Thing was, we didn't have a clue which direction the train station was in as we'd come down a different road in the taxi, so just walked in the direction we thought it was. We asked a few people which way it was and they said it was a long walk, and once we'd got ourselves properly lost amongst the rather pleasant looking snow-covered residential streets, we decided to give in and call a taxi – luckily I'd picked up a card from the taxi earlier, so phoned one from an outside an old community centre type building.

Once back at the station we were told that our train was two and a half hours late leaving New York, but they were putting on a replacement bus service back to Toronto. After a half hour wait we on our way, and got back to Toronto much earlier than we thought, about an hour and a half earlier than the train was due to be back, even if it had been on time. It was actually quite good to see a bit of Canada from a bus along the motorway instead of from a train, gave a slightly different impression of the place, especially as we moved closer to the Toronto skyline with the CN Tower standing high in the clear blue evening sky. It was tempting to go and see the view from the CN Tower on a clear evening, but we'd been up there they day before and were both tired, and we didn't want to be late for the train to Winnipeg in the morning, so went back to the hotel to crash out early again.

Tuesday 5th April 2005

Tuesday morning and it was time to head out west on the longest train journey of them all. The train to Winnipeg was due to leave Toronto at 9am and arrive in Winnipeg just before 4pm the next day, taking nearly 32 hours (Winnipeg is a further hour behind GMT being on Central Time). The train itself, known as 'the Canadian', would carry on all the way to Vancouver which takes 3 days. We would break that up with stops in Winnipeg and Jasper. We arrived at the train station in plenty of time, after paying for the extras on our bill, namely laundry and my drunken raid on the mini-bar, and were soon settled on the train ready for the big journey.

As we pulled out of Union Station I began to reflect on the four days in Toronto. It had been a good place to use as a base, especially with our hotel being so close to the train station, and we'd seen the things we'd set out to see – the CN Tower, Eaton Centre, Niagara Falls and some ice hockey. Toronto itself is a huge city, and the suburbs seemed to go on forever as the train rolled along. What struck me was that for such a large city, it never seemed overly congested, at least in the city centre for I understand the freeways get a bit congested in rush hour. Even at busy times of the working day though there never seemed to be the overcrowding that we seem to have in every town and city in England. One could read into that and say that reflects the high population density of England compared to Canada, as even the smallest of English towns seem to get congested all to easily. Toronto has a very modern and clean feel to it. It's a very cosmopolitan city as well, and has a big city feel to it with all its high rise buildings, but I never once felt the slightest bit uneasy in terms of personal security. I know we only saw a small part of the centre of Toronto and very little of the suburbs, but overall I was very impressed with it.

After about half an hour we were out of the suburbs and into the countryside, which soon became the wild forested landscape that one associates with Canada. Time for the music and I started off with some real ambient stuff, Spirit of Africa by Terry Oldfield. The music seemed to be perfect for the occasion, and captured the mood of being on a long and inspirational journey, with its gradual build up and mood enhancing ambience, reflecting the eye pleasing scenery rolling by. The area that we would be passing through on the journey to Winnipeg would include some of the finest examples of landscape that is characterised by the Canadian Shield, which is a vast horseshoe-shaped area around the Hudson Bay covering eastern and central Canada and part of the northern USA. The rocks of the Canadian Shield were formed over 500 million years ago, and due to the effects of glaciation the Canadian Shield has very thin soil with rocky outcroppings frequently showing. It is mainly undulating land with small hills and numerous lakes.

After the ambience of Terry Oldfield it was time for some other music, so I went for The Who's Ultimate collection, which I'd recently purchased and copied to the MP3 player. When it got to track 20 I immediately recognised the song from a British film which I couldn't remember, but was later informed to be Fever Pitch! The song though was Baba O'Reilly, and this above all other music I listened to on the whole trans-Canada rail trip seemed to capture the moment. The way the song builds up with more and more elements of the song blending in is just sheer magic, and was so perfect for accompanying looking out of the window at the scenery of the Canadian Shield, with thoughts of how great it was to be heading out west, travelling across a country that I'd wanted to visit for so long, that I must have played it three or four times in succession. As soon as I hear the song now I'm brought back to that train journey through rural Ontario, and you could say it's the anthem of the trip!

It was soon time for lunch and rather than have the basic sandwiches from the food counter we decided to treat ourselves to lunch in the restaurant car. It was the first time I've ever sat in a dining car on a train, and I have to say it was rather nice, most civilised! It was soup for starters followed by a main course of chicken and rice, and conversation with fellow passengers about our respective journeys whilst watching the scenery roll by. There were quite a few people there doing the full three day journey to Vancouver, which to me is a bit long, glad we had the breaks of Winnipeg and Jasper to look forward to. After lunch we were delighted to hear the announcement that the staff were organising a game of bingo in the games car! Fantastic! Bingo on the trans-Canadian, organised by the lovely Jody. There were about half a dozen of us playing, free to enter, and I was delighted to win a moose key ring, which later went to fulfil a request from my friend Chris from York (yes, the third Chris mentioned in this book!) to bring him a moose back from Canada!

After the bingo me and Chris had a game of Trivial Pursuits – Canadian version! The thing was, although we didn't have a clue with most of the questions being about Canadian news and entertainment, etc, we found that at least a quarter of the answers were either "Canada" or "Canadian"! "Which country won bronze medal for 200m swimming in the 1948 Olympics....erm, that must be Canada". Either that or it was a question starting "which Canadian Prime Minister…", which given that we only knew of two or three was a little difficult. As it was we were both tied on the last question, and Chris came back to beat me, just. It was all good fun. After that they showed a video, Dodgeball, which I'd seen before but watched again as it's a good film. I have to say that the staff on that journey were great, they made an effort to both inform people of journey based facts, as well as provide a good service and have a good laugh with us. After all the fun and games, it was time to return to our seats and chill out for a while.

I spend the next few hours reading and watching the unchanged scenery roll by until it got dark, and then we went back to the restaurant car for dinner at about 9pm. We were sat with a German girl from Frankfurt who had been studying in Montreal, but was going to Vancouver for a visit before going home. Once dinner was out the way it was time to crash out. I soon dozed off but the persistent motion of the train came to a halt for a while which woke me up, when the train stopped at a place called Hornepayne for over an hour at midnight. Every so often on these long journeys the train has to stop for refuelling and stuff, but this stop seemed to go on forever and waiting for it to move again got me irritable, so I couldn't sleep until it got going again, after which I had a solid sleep for several hours.

Wednesday 6th April 2005

I woke up at about 6-45am when the train came to a stop at a small place called Armstrong, when loads of First Nations / Native Americans / Indians got on the train. Seemed like the whole tribe, there was an endless stream of them walking past! Once young lad saw me wake up and said "sorry, for being loud", and then stayed very quiet. Most polite I thought. They were all fairly quiet and respected the fact that most people were still asleep, and got off half an hour later in a very remote village called Collins, which was no more than a group of houses spread out in a clearing in the woods. There was a number of skidoos there to collect the luggage of those getting off, as there was still quite a bit of snow on the ground there, and then we were off on our way again. By now, although still in Ontario, we were onto Central Standard Time, which is 6 hours behind UK time, and as it was daylight I stayed awake to watch the frozen landscape roll by.

We stopped at a place called Sioux Lookout at around 9am, for the usual refuelling etc. The train staff said that the place is named after a nearby hill which was used by the Ojibway tribe which was at war with the invading Sioux in the 18th century. Legend has it that the Ojibway camped at the peak of Sioux Mountain so they could see the approaching Sioux canoes from miles away, and set up a successful ambush thereby repelling the invaders. Seeing as we'd been on the train for 24 hours, I went out to get some fresh air and stretch my legs. I only walked about 100 yards, but it was nice to take some deep breaths of early morning western Ontario air. As I got to the main road at the top of the slope up from the platform, I had to laugh when I saw the sign above the place opposite – "The Looney Bin – adult education centre"! Other than that I didn't see any nearby shops open which sold newspapers or refreshments, so I went back down to the platform by which time Chris had decided to get some fresh air and said he was feeling a bit ill.

We were soon on our way again enjoying the spectacular scenery of the Canadian Shield. No huge mountains like we'd see in the Rockies, but forests, frozen lakes and rocky outcrops spread over rolling hills. It reminded me a little bit of Aberdeenshire in Scotland, where I used to live as a child, and I couldn't help comparing the journey out west to the journey through Deeside towards Ballater and Braemar. It may sound like a strange comparison but it's helped by the fact that Deeside to me is mainly childhood memories, and the constant westerly direction to eventually more rough mountainous terrain (except for Manitoba and Saskatchewan) reminded me of that. Given the slow speed of the train, I saw quite a few footprints in the snow, but no bears despite my constant scanning of the woods, although I did see some deer at one point.

The weather had become very sunny, and the snow and ice soon disappeared to give the impression that it was very warm outside. I had a sandwich and a couple of beers for lunch, and soon we were in Manitoba and the rolling tree covered hills and been largely replaced by open prairie. I'd taken loads of video clips on the phone to remember the journey by, and it hadn't been half as bad as one might expect. I actually quite enjoyed that train journey, with the constant feel of heading out further west towards more adventure, although it was a relief to hear the announcement that we'd be arriving an hour early at about 3pm. So after 31 hours on the train, we were finally in Winnipeg, halfway across Canada, and the thing that stuck us was how hot it was!

Chapter Four – Manitoba

A few weeks previously it had been -12'C in Winnipeg, something I'm not used to living in England, but now it was nearly 20'C. Winnipeg (Cree word for "muddy waters") is situated on the confluence of the Red and Assiniboine Rivers and is home to over half a million people. I'd booked the hotel when still in Toronto, the Radisson on Portage Avenue, and it was just a 15 minute walk from the train station. As we were walking up the road Chris was feeling very ill and had to stop for a rest and drink a can of coke before carrying on. It can't have been alcohol because he didn't drink anything on the train.

We were soon at the hotel though and our room number was 2006, which I instantly decided was an omen that England would win the World Cup in 2006! We were up on the 20th floor and it was quite some view from there. Winnipeg and the surrounding area is totally flat, and we could see for miles across the hot and dry looking city and beyond. Chris decided to crash out for a bit so I went to make use of the swimming pool and spa, very nice too after 31 hours on a train. There were only a couple of other people there who didn't stay for long, and it was quite relaxing. After that it was time for dinner, so we went to the hotel bar and I had a bison hot pot, which was nice. They were showing clips from Liverpool and Chelsea's Champions League victories on TSN (The Sports Network, Canada's equivalent of Sky Sports) in the bar, but our attention would soon turn to another sport as we had tickets for the Manitoba Moose v Syracuse Crunch that evening, another AHL ice hockey game which started at 6pm.

The MTS centre, where the game was being held, was just around the corner from the hotel, so once there I got a beer (Chris was having another no beer day!) and went down to our seats on the front row. The arena itself was of a similar size to Hamilton, and again only had the lower tier seating open but with a slightly larger crowd. Before the match we were reminded of the time difference from home (now 6 hours) when my friend Chris (the one who'd provided me with the England v Azerbaijan score a week earlier) phoned after being in the pub all night.

Our front row seats were soon to prove their worth when a fight broke out right in front of us. I love the way that in ice hockey that two players call a fight, drop their sticks, throw off their gloves and then batter each other with all the other players and officials stood watching. Apparently there's a saying in Canada, "I went to watch a fight and game of hockey broke out"! This one went on for over a minute, with both of them grabbing each other for balance and then getting punches in when they could. No one went down and it ended even, but provided another great addition to the video clip collection on my phone (with me shouting "go on, hit him…deck him….").

The game itself was quite entertaining but ended in a 4-3 defeat for the home side. I was surprised at how quiet the crowd were, as after what the Scottish lads at the Hamilton match were saying I thought the fans in Winnipeg would be a lot more passionate in their support, especially with the absence of a nearby NHL team due to the Winnipeg Jets franchise having moved to Phoenix in 1996 to become the Coyotes (the Moose are affiliated with the Vancouver Canucks, which isn't exactly close to Winnipeg!). All in all a good match and at least we'd now seen a couple of hockey games in Canada, not quite the NHL but the next best thing. Afterwards we were both a bit tired so went back to the hotel without having any more beers (Chris still wasn't drinking and I'd had a few at the hockey), ready for our one full day in Winnipeg before heading out further west on the Friday.

Thursday 7th April 2005

The one attraction in Winnipeg that stood out in the Rough Guide book was the Manitoba Museum, so after breakfast this is where we headed, after I had a great moment of indecision about whether to wear my coat or not due to the weather being warmer than expected, and changed my mind a couple of times before going back from reception to get it! The museum is on Rupert Avenue, not too far away from the hotel but we still managed to head in the wrong direction before asking someone. This was after crossing the junction of Portage and Main, which is reportedly the windiest corner in North America, and we could appreciate why. Even on a relatively calm and sunny day there was a strong wind blowing around the junction. I think the subway underneath is to avoid the wind, not just the traffic!

The museum itself provides a fascinating insight into the history of man and nature, with a focus on the history of Manitoba. The whole museum is set out like a walk through time, so you start off with the history of the planet and how life evolved, gradually moving through the ages until the settlement of Manitoba over the last few centuries is covered. The earth history section shows how the traces of Manitoba's geological history remain in the fossils of the Ordovician Sea, which covered the province a half-billion years ago. The wildlife displays are very impressive, and include polar bears (with the sound of a polar wind and changes in light to accompany the surrounding polar scenery), buffalo, wolves and many others, all with their natural habitats recreated around them.

The human history displays include a lot of information about the Hudson Bay Company, which had so much influence on the development of Canada, including an impressive recreation of a 17th century English waterfront with a 1970 replica of the *Nonsuch*, a two mast ketch ship which sailed from Norfolk to the Hudson Bay in 1688 in search of furs, leading to the foundation of the Hudson Bay company two years later. The replica completed the same journey in 1970 as part of the tri-centennial celebrations of the HBC before finding its home in the museum, and you are able to walk on deck and inside the ship. It seems remarkable how the journey across the Atlantic was made in a ship so small, with sleeping quarters inside for no more than six crew members, but it does seem like quite a sturdy and complete ship. The tour of the museum is completed by the urban section, which takes you through the settlement of Manitoba over the last few centuries by Europeans, which was equally fascinating.

All in all I found the museum very interesting and definitely recommend a visit to anyone with time to spare in Winnipeg. It's very educational for people of all ages, we were certainly kept interested by the various displays, but I think it's great for kids, which was reflected by the various school groups being taken round. So after two informative hours we had an afternoon in which to keep ourselves occupied before going for a good drink later on. We headed down Portage Avenue past the hotel, and went into a bar called Mumbo Jumbo just inside the Portage Place Mall for some lunch and the obligatory beer (in my case anyway!). After that we wandered through the shopping mall, looking in a number of shops, before walking back up Portage Avenue to the hotel via the Manitoba Moose souvenir shop. I bought a couple of shot glasses and t-shirts in there, and Chris had bought a couple of Moose replica shirts, adding to the ever increasing weight of our bags.

After chilling out in the hotel for a few hours it was time for dinner and some beers, and rather than go hunting for a restaurant we ate in the hotel again. It's quite a nice little restaurant in there, ten floors up with a good view of the flat landscape of Winnipeg and the surrounding area, and TSN keeping us up to date with the sports news, which was mainly hockey but also included some football (real football that is, the one that involves primarily moving a ball with one's foot, hence the name foot-ball, not throwing it and running for ten seconds before another two minute break, wearing strange looking tights, more padding than the Michelin man, and a helmet more suited to a hockey goalkeeper facing a puck at 100mph!). Anyway, I had steak and mash which was nice, don't normally eat steak but thought it would be good for a change, and so with a suitable beer base we went out to sample the nocturnal delights of Winnipeg.

We'd not had a proper drinking session since the Saturday night in Toronto, and even Chris was back on the drink tonight, so for starters we went to the Elephant and Castle pub, which is part of the Delta Winnipeg hotel on St Mary Avenue, just one block away from our hotel. It's quite a decent pub, slightly English in style but with the usual North American thing of being a bar/gill rather than just a pub, and having eaten at the hotel we sat at a couple of stools by the bar. We had a good few beers in there, talking about the trip so far, what was to come, life back home, money, sport and women. Talking of which, one of the waitresses in there was a spitting image of a girl who worked in our office, looked two thirds like her and one third like her sister who also worked there. I sent her a text message to tell her but never got a reply seeing as it was 10pm and therefore 4am back home!

After that we went to the Kings Head on Kings Street, which is another pub slightly English in character, as one would expect from the name. There are football scarves all over the pub, mostly British clubs and a few European ones. I was disappointed not to see a Darlington one there, so we thought about posting one over when we got back. They had other lower division clubs like Oxford United and Huddersfield Town, as well as bigger clubs like West Ham, Tottenham and Liverpool, and Scottish clubs like Rangers and their not very British to put it mildly (very mildly if you know my usual description of them!) Glasgow rivals. It was quite good in there, but after a few beers we went off in the search of somewhere more lively. Even though it was in the downtown area, bars were few and far between, which is generally the case in North America, unlike the UK where pubs and bars are congregated in several main areas around the city or town centre, with other pubs scattered elsewhere in the town. I guess that says something about the British drinking culture!

By now we were feeling quite lively from the beer and wanted a decent bar or club, but when some homeless type person suggested the nearby lap dancing club, it just had to be done. It wasn't too expensive to get in, the drinks were reasonable, the place was smart enough, and the girls were stunning. Obviously pretty much the only women in there would be working, so there'd be no chance of pulling, but at least there'd be plenty to look at. Some bloke got talking to Chris and when he heard we were English he decided we were from Liverpool and lived next door to Paul McCartney! Whatever!

Rather than listen to his drunken ramblings, I paid $40 (about £17) for my own private lap dance by a complete stunner, much more entertaining! No touching and in full view of everyone else, but it was good entertainment. She was beautiful. Worth telling a couple of people back home via SMS, nice for them to wake up to on their way to work. The place was okay really, no hint of trouble despite its slightly mid-west saloon type feel, but after a few more beers and then some rum the bar closed around 2am and it was time to go back to the hotel. Nowhere near as drunk as in Toronto, but drunk enough and it'd been a good night.

Friday 8th April 2005

Given our late and slightly drunken night, it was a late start to the morning, a day that would see us heading further west across Manitoba, across Saskatchewan through the night, into Alberta the next day with the much anticipated Rockies drawing closer and then into Jasper mid-afternoon. After breakfast we made use of the internet facilities to book our hotels for Jasper and Vancouver via Expedia, choosing the Whistlers Inn at Jasper and the Ramada in Vancouver. I also took the opportunity to post a message on the travel website of my friends Mel and Sue, who were on a year long trip around the world, encompassing China and south east Asia, Australia, New Zealand, some Pacific Islands, South America, Canada and the USA. They'd set up a website through STA Travel with photos, message board and map showing their current location, and it was a great way to follow their progress. We'd talked about our respective travels before they set off, and although they wouldn't be in Canada until the autumn, we hoped to meet up somewhere along the line, so maybe another trip across the Atlantic would be called for later in the year. Anyway, I posted on the message board to say that we were thoroughly enjoying Canada and were about to leave Winnipeg, the halfway point of our journey.

Once we'd checked out of the hotel just before 1pm, we couldn't think of anything to do so we walked down to the train station, even though our train wasn't due to leave until 16:55. The next few hours were spent sat in the main hall of the train station, drinking tea, reading, and waiting for time to pass. With trains being few and far between it was very quiet around the station, but it's quite a clean and pleasant building so waiting around wasn't too bad. It had been a good couple of days in Winnipeg, well worth taking the break from the train after 31 hours, good to spend time at the geographical halfway point of our journey, and good to see a city that differs somewhat from those in the east and west of Canada.

I think the main things that summarise Winnipeg are the sheer flatness of the city and the surrounding area, which means one can see for miles and miles from any of the taller buildings such as our hotel, plus the city has a feeling of being more American mid-west than Canadian, which can probably be explained by its location in respect of other Canadian cities and it's close proximity to the border with the United States (about 60 miles). The weather was also a surprise. As I've already mentioned, I'd seen weather forecasts a few weeks previously with temperatures of -12'C in Winnipeg, and was expecting it to be rather cold, even in early April. Apparently Winnipeg is often given the nickname Winter-peg due to its cold weather. But when we got there Spring was kicking in and we'd already seen on the journey so far that the frozen landscape was thawing out and recovering from the harsh Canadian winter, we just didn't expect temperatures of nearly 20'C in Winnipeg! I've since heard of people saying Winnipeg is too cold in winter and too hot in summer, which I guess is due to its continental climate giving more extremes of weather.

Our train arrived long before the 16:55 departure time, but we weren't allowed to go through the gate and board until about half an hour before departure, by which time we'd become a little frustrated by the waiting around when the train was sat there, but I guess they have their system and had to service the train first. Once on we got a couple of seats near the front of a carriage, with a few other people scattered about. We were soon on our way out of Winnipeg, the start of a 22 hour journey to Jasper, which would begin with the endless flat plains of Manitoba. I'm sure it's no coincidence that the train travels through Saskatchewan at night, as it's more of the same with very flat scenery all around. As the train pulled out of Winnipeg we saw the Red River at flood level, and the scenery then gave way to open prairie with bits of flood water accumulation here and there.

There were a few other younger people on the train this time, and we soon got talking to a few of them, notably Ray from somewhere in Ontario who was on his way to Edmonton, where he was taking over the editorial of a local weekly paper, and Phil from Ottawa who was on his way to Banff where he'd be working with his brother for the summer. Me, Chris and Ray ended up getting a few beers in, sitting down in the observation car for a while, and talking mostly about sport. As far as football was concerned Ray was a Tottenham fan, and we told him about us following Darlington, and some of the many away trips I'd been on with both Darlington and England. We all agreed that American Football was rubbish to say the least, but that hockey was a decent sport, although he wasn't too keen on cricket. I'm not a massive fan of cricket but like to see England do well and it's also one of the great English traditions. As far as hockey was concerned he was a fan of the Ottawa Senators, provincial rivals of the great Toronto Maple Leafs, and we talked about the current NHL lockout. It made a change to be talking to other passengers in more detail, and getting their angle on life, rather than just the polite conversation we'd had so far on the trains.

When things went quiet I couldn't help coming out with my favourite line at the time – "just think, this is the further west that I've ever been" – before repeating it again ten seconds later, and again, and again. Soon did everyone's heads in with that one! Once it got dark we crossed over into Saskatchewan, and because they don't operate Daylight Savings Time in that province, we had to adjust our watches back one hour, which at least meant we wouldn't have to put them back when crossing into Alberta and Mountain Time, as they do operate Daylight Savings Time! That put us 7 hours behind UK time (British Summer Time).

That was the seventh time zone change since leaving home less than two weeks previously and there'd be more to come. We'd gone from Greenwich Meantime to British Summer Time when in London, BST to Newfoundland Standard Time at St John's, then to Atlantic Standard Time in Halifax, Eastern Standard Time on the way to Montreal, Eastern Daylight Savings Time in Toronto, Central DST in Manitoba, Central Standard Time in Saskatchewan, and we still had to change to Mountain DST (which didn't actually involve a change!), Pacific DST before finally going back to British Summer Time when we got back to the UK.

At about 9pm Central something or other time, we had one of the half hour stops in the small town of Melville, and with quite a few people getting off for a smoke break (VIA Rail trains are thankfully non-smoking) I thought it'd be a good idea to stretch my legs and get some fresh air. As I was stood there talking to Ray, I had the bright idea of going for a beer and finding a cash machine, as my cash supply was getting a bit low, and beer is always a good idea on such occasions. So myself and Ray walked a few hundred yards into town, found an ATM so got that sorted, then went looking for a bar being careful not to go too far from the train.

As we were walking down the road we walked past a bunch of kids in their early to mid teens, to whom Ray said "hi guys" and got the same in reply without any hint of aggression or animosity. I couldn't help thinking that the same thing in the UK would be met by a torrent of abuse from a group of young teenagers. Anyway, we found a bar around the corner and went in for a quick beer, nice enough small town bar with a few people in, but with the train to catch we downed the beers in about 3 minutes before going back to the train. Nice beer, and at least I can say I've had a beer in Saskatchewan and got to stretch my legs before we got going again.

One of the problems with where we were sat on the train was that someone was sat behind my seat with a small child, and it seemed that the child must have wet itself or something, as I kept getting smells of urine, and once that aroma is in your nostrils it's hard to forget. On top of that the kid kept crying and screaming, which prompted quite a few people to spend a large part of the evening down in the observation car or the small café area. I even tried sleeping in the observation car but it gets very cold up there (it's half a carriage raised above the rest with half a dozen steps leading up to it, and has a glass roof), so I ended up going back to my seat at about midnight near the minging horrible smell and the occasional crying of the kid. I may be a bit insensitive as I don't currently have any kids of my own, but surely it's not right to take such young children (I'd guess about 18months old) on such a long train journey.

Anyway, when the train pulled into Saskatoon at about 1am someone got off across the aisle and slightly further forward and I took the chance to move seats. My MP3 player and Vicks inhaler helped with the problem a bit, but I was probably being a bit fussy and paranoid about it all looking back. The conductor had wanted to sit a new passenger where I'd moved to and asked me to move back to my seat, but I just acted sleepier than I was and said I sleep better on the left hand side of the train. There was no way I was moving back after all that, and rather than create a fuss he gave the new passenger my old seat, in front of the women with small child. And soon, finally, I dropped off to sleep for several hours, nice and comfortable apart from the odd noise from the kid, but even they slept eventually.

Chapter Five – Alberta

Saturday 9th April 2005

I woke up sometime after 6am, just as we were approaching Edmonton where we were due to arrive at 7am. We were now in Alberta, which is on Mountain Time, but as I've said we'd already gone back one hour due to Saskatchewan not operating Daylight Savings Time as Alberta does, so no need for another watch adjustment. I'd had a good few hours sleep, and once at Edmonton I took the opportunity to go for a walkabout and get some fresh air, as did most other passengers. It's a very small train station and seems to be some way out of the city, but had basic facilities so I had a quick wash to wake myself up a bit. Ray went off on his way and we wished each other well, and I got talking to a couple of older Canadians who'd been on the train, one of whom gave me a Canadian flag pin badge, which was nice. We were at Edmonton for about an hour, it gave us a good break from the journey but we were soon on our way west again. With Saskatchewan behind us and now Edmonton, all thoughts now would turn to the Rockies.

The Trans-Canada Rail Guide by Melissa Graham was proving to be very useful, but it would be of particular use as we approached the Rocky Mountains. The book describes the change of scenery over the miles, so I knew roughly when to expect my first sight of the Rockies and when we would be travelling through the mountains themselves. I would definitely recommend everyone who is planning on travelling across Canada by train to buy this book, as it proves to be an invaluable guide. By late morning I was expecting to get my first glimpse of the Rockies and was sat up in the observation car with my camera waiting to see them appear on the horizon. The anticipation amongst the other passengers was quite tangible. Whether people had been on the train since Toronto, Winnipeg, Edmonton, or anywhere in between, everyone was looking forward to seeing the majestic beauty of the Rocky Mountains.

At around midday I got my first glimpse of the mountains, and it sounds strange but it was quite a buzz to finally see them appear on the horizon, a line of snow capped mountains sticking up high over the plains and the tree covered foothills in front of them. We were probably about a hundred miles away from the Rockies at that point, and after the initial excitement and picture taking I went back to my seat for a while. The scenery soon changed from the open plains to more and more trees, the elevation was gradually increasing and soon we were going over and around tree covered rolling hills. The scenery became quite spectacular with the view of forested landscape giving way to rivers and canyons, with the mountains looming ever closer. Whereas the forests of Ontario seemed much more mixed with a higher proportion of deciduous trees, the forests here were nearly all conifers and therefore greener at the time of year. At around 1-30pm we arrived at Hinton, which is often described as the gateway to the Rockies, and from here on it we would be in the Rockies for real, just an hour to Jasper to go but it would be the most spectacular hour of the whole train journey so far.

Once out of Hinton the scenery soon became more dramatic, at times passing along the edge of high rocky slopes on one side with endless forest on the other, and at other times we'd be passing along the edge of a vast sandy flood plain with mountains all around. At one point I saw a lone wolf running along next to an icy river, as we pushed onwards through the mountainous scenery. The whole view all around was of pure beauty, a true feast for the eyeballs, and it was this that I'd been looking forward to seeing for so long. Of course, we were still on the train, and this being Canada meant that the view out of the left hand side window I was looking out of was suddenly interrupted by a goods train going the other way, which must have been at least two miles long and left me looking out of the other side of the train for ten minutes. It gave me the chance to check out a different viewpoint for my photos, which I was alternating between my camera, phone and video clips on my phone. We also passed another VIA rail train at one point, travelling from Vancouver to Toronto, the two trains slowing right down to almost walking pace, allowing the respective crews to see each other and have a quick chat over the radio. We were now well and truly in the Canadian Rockies, and soon arrived in the small town of Jasper, at the heart of the Jasper National Park.

Before getting off the train we were talking to Phil from Ottawa who was due to catch a bus to Banff, but he didn't have a clue when the bus left and suspected he'd missed it. I said that we'd be in the Whistlers Inn and if he had any problems with the bus then to come and meet us in there. Once off the train we quickly saw where our hotel was, basically just across the road from the small train station. I had to stop though and take in the view, and my first word was a simple "wow". You always know that you're in an amazing place on this planet when you stop, look all around, and just say that small word in response to the views around you. Jasper townsite is in a truly beautiful location. High snow covered mountains all around, endless conifer trees on the lower slopes, and to make it better it was a nice clear day with just a few scattered clouds. It was fresh but certainly not cold. I was feeling very positive at the thought of spending five days in Jasper.

Once at the hotel we checked in and went to our room to dump our bags off, very nice room with the standard two double beds, table, TV and decent bathroom, and as we said we'd be in the bar to meet Phil in case he'd missed his bus we went straight down there. I was surprised to see people smoking in there after getting used to non-smoking pubs for the previous two weeks, but it turned out that the smoking ban in Alberta was being strengthened the following week and that pub would be joining most of the others in the town who'd already banned it totally. The smoke wasn't too bad though. There was no Alexander Keith's at the bar so I went for a Kokanee, a 'glacier beer' which is brewed in British Columbia. Maybe it was habit which kept the Keith's at number one spot, but the Kokanee was a very close second, it's a lovely beer. To accompany the beer I had an elk burger for a late lunch, which was nice although I wasn't expecting all the chips as well so I left half of them. I sent a text to my parents telling them of my elk burger, and got a reply from my cousin Katie saying they were all having a late meal in the Tithe Bar in Northallerton. That all seemed so far away as I sat in a town which again marked the furthest west I'd ever been, and with England being 7 hours ahead of Jasper time it was gone 10pm back home.

As we were sat there Phil came in, he'd missed his bus after all, telling us that it had left at 8-30 am - he was only six hours late! When he went to the bar he got ID'd but didn't have any on him, and being only 20 and young looking he wasn't getting served, even though the drinking age is 18 in Alberta. As Chris wasn't eating he went out with Phil and I said I'd see them either outside or back up at the room. After leaving half of the chips I went outside but couldn't see them, so went up to the room and found they weren't there. They soon turned up though and were loaded with supplies, a crate of beer, a half bottle of rum and a half bottle of whisky. It looked like a lively Saturday night was on the cards then! We told Phil he was welcome to crash out on the floor for the night, so we all got showered and changed, listened to various tunes but mainly Oasis, made a good dent in the beer supply and then went out for the night at around 6pm. Myself and Chris certainly hadn't fallen out over the two weeks that we'd been away, but at times there's only so much conversation that two mates can think of so it was good to have someone else join us for a night or two.

We turned left out of the Whistlers Inn down Patricia Street, which is full of small shops and restaurants, and went into the L&W restaurant opposite the end of the street. The elk burger was a few hours ago by now, but ruled out the need for a starter. It was quite well set out in there with plants all over the place and the tables well spread out, and we were seated near the window with a view of the mountains that tower over the town. The food in there was excellent, I opted for British Colombia salmon which was gorgeous, and the other two enjoyed their food as well. After the food we sat outside the back of the restaurant, even though it was a bit cool the sun was still shining and it was nice to take in the scenery and have a relaxing drink after the meal. I've mentioned before the comparisons with Aberdeenshire where I lived as a young child, and I couldn't help comparing Jasper to Ballater, which is on the way out to Braemar. It's on a completely different scale, but new places usually remind you of somewhere else in the world.

As we were sat there I couldn't help think that Phil was just like our friend back home Nooney, both in appearance and behaviour. The same disorganisation such as missing a bus by six hours and losing his phone charger on the train, the same rucksack full of CDs, the same untidiness with his possessions, the same mannerisms and humour, just a bit younger and Canadian. So Phil became known as the Canadian Nooney! I told the real Nooney via text and he said to pass on his regards to his Canadian counterpart. He'd been with us for a few days during the World Cup in France, and I couldn't help making comparisons to that trip.

We got talking about Phil's plans for the next day, and he was unsure of whether there were any buses the next day (that's what I mean about disorganisation!) and suggested that we hire a car and drive there for a night out. Chris was well up for it and despite having the hotel room in Jasper, I was up for it as well. We'd only need a few things and would return to Jasper on Monday. It would be my first chance to drive abroad (other than 5 miles in a British car in rural Norway) and would be an adventure. We had no idea where Banff was in relation to Jasper, I actually thought it was north at the time, but we'd get a map and sort a car out the next day. Phil said his brother had been working there for a while and knew loads of people and the best places to go for a drink. It all sounded rather fun, so the road trip and a night out in Banff was on for the next day.

Once the sun had set it got a bit cooler, so we paid our bill, leaving a generous tip and thanking the waitress saying we'd be back again later in the week, and headed back down Patricia Street to find a bar. Given Phil's inability to be served alcohol in the Whistlers Inn, we couldn't go in there so instead went into O Shea's bar which formed part of the Athabasca Hotel, just across the road from the Whistlers. There were a couple of folk singers in there for a while, just to give the place a nice touristy feel, then we ended up playing a few games of pool (or rather we watched Phil's attempts at being a pool shark). They seem to have some kind of weird rules in Canada where fluke shots aren't allowed or something, plus all the pockets and balls are a bit bigger.

We got talking to a lovely girl called Alison who was from Edmonton and was working at the nearby Marmot Basin resort. Unfortunately she wasn't staying for too long as she said she was drunk enough after four beers, but we said we'd hopefully meet up on the Monday once we got back from Banff. We also got talking to a lad called Cy (short for Cyan as in the light blue colour apparently) who was a pilot and was wearing his pilot uniform (but with jeans instead of black trousers!), saying it was good for pulling the ladies. He was about my age (32), from Calgary, was half-Irish, had studied in Newcastle, and had a weird accent. After a few more beers in there the nightclub part of the hotel opened up so we went though there.

It was quiet in there to start with but soon filled up, the beers were flowing well and we all ended up being quite drunk to say the least. We told Cy about the Banff trip and he said that rather than hire a car he would drive us up there, which suited me as I didn't have to worry about driving and could drink a bit more. He also said he was a Glasgow Celtic supporter and a Fenian (Irish republican), which is completely the opposite to my views on Scottish football and Northern Irish politics to put it mildly, but I thought what the hell we're on holiday and he was a good laugh, so any such differences of opinion was put to one side. The night became a blur in the end, all of us (the Banff Road Trip Four) were off talking to various people and attempting to dance and were drinking for England (or Canada!). I remember Chris at one point looking as if he was thinking for ages about something to say, and then he just said "I'm smashed", which kind of summed the night up. I went back to the hotel shortly afterwards, at about 1am, and drank some rum before passing out. Chris came back not long after apparently, and Phil said he had to ask reception for another key, as we were well asleep when he came back at around 4am. All in all a good night, and we had a road trip to Banff to look forward to.

Sunday 10th April 2005

We'd arranged to meet Cy outside the front of the hotel at around 11am, in theory giving us time to get over our hangovers, but that didn't quite work out due to the amount of alcohol consumed. The three of us went to a local shop to get some kind of breakfast, and then waited for Cy to turn up. He arrived sometime after 11am, and was still wearing the same pilot shirt and tie he'd had on the night before, which amused us a little. We were soon on the road to Banff, finally leaving Jasper at about midday, and searching through Cy's tape collection was hard work, ending up with some Johnny Cash to start us off with ("....and it burns, burns, burns, the ring of fire, the ring of fire, der der-der der-der der der der"). It seemed an appropriate choice of music for the journey and surroundings though. The road trip had begun.

After two weeks of train travel, except the bus back to Toronto from Niagara Falls, it was good to be travelling by car. The journey from Jasper to Banff is about 180 miles, most of which is along the Icefields Parkway, and it is often described as one of the most scenic highways in the world. Even after just a few miles, it was clear to see that there was no arguing with that description. The beginning of the journey was mostly driving through the forested landscape with the mountains looming over us, but the elevation of the road soon changed more in line with the hills and we were offered stunning views across the valleys. Being sat in the front I had a better view as well, seeing the road unfold in front of us with more and more mountains appearing in the background. This is what we'd come to see in Canada, this is the type of scenery that you see in all the guidebooks, and it's true to say that every view was a picture postcard. This is the one image that I described at the beginning of this book, the one that stands out above the rest, the one of dramatic, stunning, mountainous scenery, with immense forests interspersed with lakes, an image of pure beauty and freedom. And just to top that image, much of the landscape was still covered in snow. It was absolutely beautiful.

We stopped at a lay-by to admire the view for about quarter of an hour and have a toilet stop, before carrying on along the Icefields Parkway. The road took us past the Columbia Icefields, which is located on the boundary of the Jasper and Banff National Parks. The Icefields is one of the largest accumulations of ice and snow south of the Arctic Circle, covering an area of about 200 square miles. The continuous accumulation of snow feeds eight major glaciers including the Athabasca, Dome, and Stutfield Glaciers, all visible from the Icefields Parkway. Melt water from the Columbia Icefields feeds streams and rivers that pour into the Arctic, Atlantic, and Pacific oceans. Unfortunately we didn't have the time (or energy!) to spend the necessary hour or two visiting the Columbia Icefields Visitors Centre, opposite which lies the Athabasca Glacier, and we didn't expect to be particularly energetic on our return journey after a night out in Banff, but at least we'd seen it.

Further on we stopped at the Saskatchewan River Crossing, where there was a shop, restaurant, accommodation and fuel. A service station in other words, but to call it such would probably put the wrong image in your mind! This place is tasteful and fits in with the surrounding area. We took the opportunity to have some lunch, before filling up with petrol and resuming the journey, this being about the halfway point of the journey and the only place to get petrol for another 80 miles. After a further refreshment stop just outside of Lake Louise, when I was informed by Cy that we'd actually been travelling south and not north as I'd thought (I wondered why the sun was in the wrong direction for so long!), we arrived in Banff at around 4pm.

We didn't have a clue where to go so parked the car in a car park and walked back down Lynx Street where we'd seen some hotels. After a few hundred yards we found the Homestead Inn, situated right next to Melissa's bar and restaurant, and that seemed ideal so we booked ourselves in there. It was more of a motel type place with our room being out the back, and once we'd booked in Phil went off to find his brother and we went back to get the car and dump our bags in the room. There would only be the three of us staying there and Cy said he'd sleep on the floor, so we just got a twin room which kept the cost down. Before driving back to the hotel we had a quick drive around the town, and Cy showed us the famous Banff Springs Hotel, a beautiful and massive hotel built in 1888 in a style that looks like a bit like a castle in Scotland.

Tempting though it was to start on the beer straight away, Chris and Cy were knackered and crashed out for a bit which left me watching the boring TV and looking at the Banff tourist map we'd picked up from reception. The first thing I noticed was how nearly every street was named after an animal or if not, a geographical feature. There's Lynx Street where we were, Bear Street, Wolf Street, Elk Street, Cougar Street, Cave Street, and, I'm delighted to say, Beaver Street. What caught my eye however was the name of a nearby lake – Lake Minnewanka! "We're going there before we leave", I said. We weren't leaving Banff without a photo of the sign for Lake Minnewanka!

The other two finally livened up and we went next door to Melissa's at about 6pm for some food and drink. Still no word from Phil, who had my phone number, and as we had his bag in our room we couldn't really go far. Melissa's has a restaurant downstairs and a bar upstairs which is where we went, and you can also get food up there so after a few beers we got hungry and ordered some food. I went for the deep pan pizza. What I got was a deep pan pizza, but the deepest deep pan pizza I have ever seen in my life! The pizza, although only about seven inches across, must have been about three inches deep! The thing was it was that nice I ate it all and ended up being so stuffed that I was struggling with the beer. After our considerable beer base we went back next door to the hotel for a bit, when Phil turned up with his brother and friend to get his bag. Although Phil was quite small, being about 5' 7" and slim, his brother was more like 6' 3" and well built, complete opposite. They said they'd be going to the Rose & Crown pub, so we said we'd meet them up there.

As we walked up the road to the Rose & Crown, Cy was telling us that bears often come into towns like Banff and Jasper, and went on to tell us about how a friend of his was attacked by a bear when out cycling through the woods, but fortunately survived. So for the rest of the night I was busy checking the streets making sure there were no bears wandering around looking for a nice feed after coming out of hibernation! The bear proof bins that they have everywhere have apparently helped reduce the number of occasions when bears search for waste food in towns, these being metal bins which have a covered catch to put your hand in to open the lid. I wonder how long it will take bears to evolve and suss those out! As for the Rose & Crown, we felt a little bit old in there, with most people there being in their late teens or early twenties. After a while we went to the other part of the pub which had a live band playing, a more mixed crowd and comfy seats but it was a touch loud, so we could barely hear each other. Is it me or is music in pubs getting louder nowadays?! I like music but not too loud, and often have trouble hearing people in loud pubs ("Eh? What?"). Maybe I'm getting old!

No sign of Phil and his brother in there, so after a while we went up the road and found a club called Aurora. I wasn't too fussed about going, being a bit bloated from the pizza and beers, but a few rums and tequilas soon sorted that out. We found Phil in the small room which was allocated to smoking, so despite my lack of tolerance of the smell we spent much of the night in there. Chatted to a few nice girls, but never really got anywhere in that sense. It was a good night in there though, and as I went looking for a girl from Edmonton I'd been talking to they called last orders, so me and Cy got double rums in to finish the night off with. The thing I noticed outside the club was the general feeling of high spirits and lack of any sort of confrontation as you often get in England after clubs and pubs close, but then I guess Banff is a small tourist town. I still had no idea where Banff was on a map, but a mini bus of people going back to Calgary made me realise it couldn't be far from there.

We walked back towards the hotel stopping at the pizza shop, I wasn't hungry after the earlier two foot deep pizza, so just bought some water, but Chris ordered a pizza, and we walked back to the hotel, with my plan being to let any bears have the pizza and leg it! Didn't see any though, and despite all the booze we'd had we were in need of more! No chance of getting any though, so had to make do with the pizza and ended up talking politics and all sorts until 4am, before finally crashing out.

Monday 11th April 2005

We all felt rough to say the least and by mid-morning we were back on the road to Jasper. Of course we had one thing to do first, and that was find a signpost to Lake Minnewanka, and after a short drive we found the required signpost, took a few photos, and then set off on the drive back to Jasper. As with the drive down to Banff we were amazed at the scenery, which became even nicer when there was some light snow falling, and again I commented on every view being a post card view. Due to there being no radio reception for much of the journey, we were relying on Cy's tape collection again, some more Johnny Cash and some CCR (Creedance Clearwater Revival).

The only thing about the journey was that there were so few signposts saying how far places were, but I guess the amazement of the scenery usually makes one forget about that. It's easy to forget just how remote the area is as you travel along in the car, admiring the scenery. There's literally nothing in terms of human occupation for mile upon mile, complete contrast to England where even in the more remote countryside there's a farm or small village after a few miles. It really is beautiful though, and I can't emphasise enough just how stunning the scenery along the Icefields Parkway is.

We stopped for a quick stretch of the legs and to take some scenic pictures, and again at the Saskatchewan River Crossing for some lunch, and got back to Jasper mid-afternoon. Once in Jasper Cy had to head back to work over at Hinton, so we bid farewell and went back to our room in the Whistlers Inn for a while. After two heavy nights drinking we were both feeling rather rough to say the least. We went for a short walk around the town, found the internet café and browsed various websites for a while to catch up on football scores etc, had a couple of beers in the Whistlers, and were both crashed out in the room by 7pm.

Before doing so I booked us a flight by float plane from Vancouver to Victoria (on Vancouver Island) for the Saturday, having seen their details on the internet before going and printing off the contact details in case we decided to do that, which we did. The flight with West Coast Air would leave Vancouver Sea Plane terminal at 10am and we would get back from Victoria at 5-30pm, with the flight taking half an hour. That would give us Friday to explore Vancouver, Saturday in Victoria, Saturday night in Vancouver before going to the airport on Sunday. It had been very much a day of recovery, feeling more like a Sunday than anything, but we still had two whole days left in Jasper to do more. It had certainly been a mad weekend, and it had been a good laugh with both Phil and Cy.

Tuesday 12th April 2005

Tuesday 11th April and we had less than a week left of our trip. We'd certainly done, seen and drank a lot in the previous two weeks, but still had the Jasper area to explore before moving onto Vancouver and Victoria, with our flight back from Vancouver being the following Sunday. After a delightful Spanish omelette for breakfast in the hotel restaurant, we went for a walk down to the Sundog Tours adventure company along Connaught Drive. I'd seen this place on the internet before going, and had ideas of doing all sorts, such as snowmobiling, guided walking, flying and taking the cable car up Whistlers Mountain. The problem was the time of year. There was no longer enough snow for winter sports, but the cable car up Whistlers wasn't open until the week after. Furthermore it turned out that the only local pilot who was flying wasn't flying as his son had just died. Tragic to say the least. We had the option of a helicopter flight but would have had to hire a car and drive back to the Athabasca glacier to do so. So in the end we settled for the wildlife tour, which would be a guided tour of the area in a car (people carrier type thing) with various stops along the way.

It was disappointing not to be going for a flight over the Rockies, but at least we had the float plane to look forward to which would be an experience in itself. We had to wait an hour or so before the wildlife tour was due to start, so just wandered around aimlessly for a while, looking in some souvenir shops, before sitting on the bench outside Sundog Tours waiting for time to pass. In a place like Jasper it's nice to sit around and take in the scenery, breathe in the fresh air and just chill out, without any stress whatsoever. The great thing about Jasper is that it has all of the beautiful scenery that Banff has, but it's not as commercialised and full of tourists and associated traffic. There are still plenty of tourists in Jasper, and it has enough to keep you entertained for a few days, but it's a lot more laid back than Banff, and has more character than Banff. Jasper is a town in itself due to the railway, whereas Banff has primarily developed due to tourism. Both fantastic and beautiful places, but Jasper is my personal preference.

The origins of Jasper goes back to 1813 when the North West Company built a supply depot at nearby Brule Lake, up towards Hinton, which was named Jasper House after clerk Jasper Hawes. This was abandoned in 1884 due to the decline of the fur trade, but after Jasper Forest Park was established in 1907, later to become Jasper National Park in 1930, and the Grand Trunk Pacific Railway reached Fitzhugh station in 1911 (renamed Jasper in 1913), the townsite was established around the divisional point of the railway and the first major building constructed was what is now the Jasper Information Centre, which was originally used for park administration and a small museum. Jasper nowadays is still remote even in the age of the internet and modern travel, so it's fascinating to imagine what it was like when the town was first established nearly a century ago.

Joining me and Chris on the Wildlife Tour was the guide, two Japanese girls in their late teens or early twenties, and a middle aged gentleman who we picked up from his accommodation elsewhere in the town. The main hope for the tour was to see a bear, which had eluded us so far, but at the very least we'd see lots more of the delightful scenery of the surrounding area with very little effort. I was a little apprehensive about seeing a bear, especially with it being spring and the time of year when they come out of hibernation looking for a good feed. Once we were all on board we first took the road north west of the town up to Pyramid Lake, which was still frozen over but starting to thaw, with good views of Pyramid Mountain in the background. We stopped by some attractive looking chalets next to the lake where the guide told us that Pyramid Mountain was made out of quartz, as opposed to the limestone which many of the surrounding mountains were. I was more concerned about bears though and he said that at this time of year they are coming down from hibernation in the mountains to the lower slopes in search of food, and are often seen around the townsite, which had me scouring the woods even more for the sight of a bear. Still no joy though. We then headed back through the town and went east of Jasper up towards Maligne Lake.

First stop after only a few miles was the Maligne Canyon, where we parked up and then went for a walk through the woods, following a path along a steep slope. I still found myself scouring the woods for bears, but to no avail. As we walked along the path the view over the trees was magnificent, seeing right across the valley to the mountains on the other side of Jasper, which provided an opportunity to take some more photos. This is what the Rockies are all about, seeing miles of trees all around, with tree covered slopes across the wide open valley leading up to snow covered mountains.

We only went as far as the first bridge some half a mile along the path, which surprised me as I was expecting a longer walk, although it's quite fascinating looking down from the small wooden footbridge which crosses over part of the canyon where we were. A wooden sign gave some information on the formation of the canyon, which was quite interesting. It seemed funny how there were trees growing from every available outcrop of rock on the near vertical slopes, which reminded me somewhat of the same thing I'd seen at Frafjord in Norway the previous year, where trees appear on the most unexpected places on the steep hill side. Still no sign of a bear and we were soon back in the car and on our way up the Maligne Lake road.

Next stop was Medicine Lake, which is about another ten miles up the road. The guide explained that the lake is connected to a vast underground water system which causes huge fluctuations in the depth of the lake. In late spring and early summer the lake is full, fuelled by the melt water from the all hills and mountains all around, but by winter the lake is almost empty after being drained like a huge bath tub during the autumn. At the time we were there the water level was very low, and it looked a bit like some English reservoirs in summer, with much of the lake bed visible. Apparently wolves in the region make it work for their hunting needs and have been known to chase caribou into the muck so they'll get stuck.

The guide pointed out a bald eagle sat in the top of a tree near the lake, which we all got to see through binoculars. It wasn't doing an awful lot but it was good to see some more wildlife that one doesn't see at home, and made a change from seeing a grouse or pheasant on the North Yorkshire Moors anyway! We didn't walk beyond the small lay-by area, but it was nice to just take in the surroundings and appreciate the pristine beauty of it all. Despite the low water level it was a magnificent view from the end of the lake, with its rocky shores leading up to gentle tree-covered slopes, giving way to steep, near vertical, rocky mountainsides. The fascinating thing about Medicine Lake is that no one knows where the underground water system actually drains the water to. Various experiments using dyes have resulted in the water being tracked to places miles apart and days apart, so it must be a truly vast underground drainage system down there.

We were soon on our way again, and with the increase in altitude came an increase in the amount of snow left in the woods around us. As well as cheerily informing us that the outside temperature was dropping, the guide told us that the air is drier up in the Rockies, which people from maritime climates tend to notice. Being from the UK, with its lovely damp climate, I had to agree, the air did seem noticeably drier, not so that it was a problem, but definitely noticeable. That's one of the things I don't like about the UK climate, damp in the winter and humid in the summer, so it was good to have a break from that. After about another 15 miles from Medicine Lake we finally came to Maligne Lake.

This marked the end of the road, the only way ahead was by dirt track or canoe, so for us on the lazy tour it was a case of getting out and having

15 minutes in the cold to enjoy the scenery. The temperature had dropped to 2'C and there was snow all around, in complete contrast to 25 miles back down the road in Jasper where it had all melted. Much of the lake itself was still frozen but it was a beautiful site. Maligne Lake is 14 miles from end to end and is the longest natural lake in the Rockies, surrounded by a ring of mountains which are capped with snow all year round. After we'd taken in enough refreshing cold air we began the 25 mile drive back to Jasper. I'd still not seen any bears, despite my constant scouring of the trees as we drove along, but we did see a few elk and some large sheep which looked like they'd been cross-bred with lama!

In no time we were back in Jasper and the tour was over. I was a bit disappointed not to have seen any bears but had thoroughly enjoyed the excursion. It's a nice easy way to take in the scenery without worrying about where you're going, as well as being told everything there is to know about the wildlife, vegetation and geology along the way. The same trip could easily be done if you were to hire a car, but you'd be advised to have a map and some background knowledge first to make it worthwhile. The easy option suited us fine though and was an enjoyable couple of hours. I'd certainly like to do the both the Pyramid Lake drive and the Maligne Lake drive again when it's a bit warmer, spend a bit more time, and possibly do some canoeing on one of the lakes. It really is beautiful up there, just what you would expect of the Canadian Rockies.

With the tour over we spent about half an hour looking at a few shops and buying various souvenirs and presents, before doing the inevitable and going to the pub. Different one this time though, the Downstream Bar further down Connaught Drive, past our hotel. The bar was downstairs and wasn't very busy, had a pleasant décor and they were playing the Bob Marley Legend album. Perfect place to rediscover my taste for beer after a couple of days absence! By now it was 6pm, 1am back home which made me ask my dad why he was still up when I got a text message from him! I told him we'd been sampling some more of the delightful scenery and I was now sampling some more of the delightful beer to the sounds of Bob. Just had a couple in there, nice and chilled out, but it got me in the mood for a few more beers, so we went back to the hotel to dump our souvenirs off, quick change and out again.

Chris was having another one of his non-drinking days so it was just me on the beer. First port of call was O Sheas, scene of Saturday's colossal session, and I was kind of hoping to see Alison in there who'd we'd been talking to on the Saturday, but she wasn't in and it was very quiet in there. We had some dinner in there and then went back over to the Whislters Inn, where we spent ages playing pool. Chris kept beating me as usual, and I still couldn't get used to the strange Canadian rules of no fluke shots allowed, what is that all about?! The bar slowly filled up and some others came and joined us, a lad called Ally who lived locally, was from Quebec originally and was bi-lingual, a lass called Shannon who was quite nice but with Ally, and Ally's mate who's name I can't remember.

Later another lad came in who I immediately thought was extremely obnoxious and arrogant, and I have to admit for the first time in ages I was tempted to express my feelings of animosity in a non-verbal method, if you know what I mean. The others were feeling the same, particularly Ally's mate, then I realised that Ally knew him so I decided to humour this lad, who turned out to be called Andy. He was just being daft but unintentionally winding some people up the wrong way, but me being me ended up having a proper good laugh with him and all previous thoughts were long forgotten. As it turned out the night became just as blurry as the Saturday and Sunday nights combined, Chris went up to bed at midnight, Ally and Shannon went off home, Andy went off, I ended up talking to God knows who and got back to the room at 2am. I remember sitting at the desk and drinking some rum, then some water at some point, sitting on the bed, then next thing I was waking up feeling very, very rough! Apparently, according to Chris, I came into the room, spat water over the table, fell out of bed and just said "bugger" and lay there for ages, put music on at 4am, and had a go at Chris for being boring when he told me to turn it off! Oh what a night!

Wednesday 13th April 2005

When I awoke Chris was gone, it was midday and my head was in bits! Still, last full day in Jasper and I wasn't going to waste it, so got showered and dressed, went next door to Smittys, on the other side of the hotel, for the usual omelette breakfast, and then went for my bright idea amazing hangover cure – a bike ride! I'd wanted to hire a bike the day before but as Chris can't actually ride a bike I didn't bother! So with him having gone for walk about town with his clear head, I decided to hire a bike and have a ride about town and beyond to try and clear my head. I'd not ridden a bike for ages and my head really was in bits when I went into the bike shop, then of course once when I was going on the bike I had to remember that they drive on the wrong side of the road, which made the first junction confusing given my state of mind! Still, my bright idea was in action and I was off and away.

I couldn't be bothered with anything too energetic, didn't fancy going off road, no bears today please my head's in bits, so just set off down Connaught Drive, which was pleasant enough. I decided to film a video clip as I was cycling along out of the town, commenting "well…here I am, riding a bike out of Jasper. This is what I call a hangover cure. Beautiful scenery". Once at the end of that road I took a right and cut across the main road, over some rough grass towards a closed looking hotel, then back up on the main road. That was my off-road bit done! The main road was the Highway 16 which links Vancouver to Edmonton, cutting through the heart of the Canadian Rockies, so there was a bit of traffic but not too much really.

At times there wouldn't be a vehicle in sight, and it was nice just taking in the scenery, looking at the straight road in front of me. I wasn't sure but correctly guessed that the road followed adjacent to Jasper which was over the embankment next to the road, and I would get back into the town at the far end where we'd come in by car previously. The only thing that concerned me was what to do if a bear appears, especially as I was now going uphill. Let's just say I got up that hill a bit quicker than I would do normally with a hangover like that! I was soon back in town and rode around a few more streets before taking the bike back to the shop, having had about an hour on it. It was a great bike with suspension and everything, very new, and it made me want to get one when I got back home. It had also cleared my head somewhat, although not totally and I was still feeling a bit rough. Very enjoyable though and I'm glad I did it.

Back to the hotel and Chris still wasn't there, but turned up after I'd been lying on the bed for ten minutes. I told him that I'd been out on the bike to clear my head, and he told me he'd been for a walkabout as I wasn't responding to anything when he got up, and he told me of my drunken entrance and fall from my bed the night before. It's funny, I'd been wondering why my clothes and bag next to the bed were looking severely flattened! I was in no mood for drinking, nor was Chris who was saving it for the weekend, so we went for another delightful meal at L&Ws where we'd eaten on Saturday. I struggled with the one beer that I did have, and the sun was blinding me through the window, but the food was nice. In a way it was good to have the last meal in Jasper where we'd had the first (excluding the elk burger late lunch!). Without the desire to drink we just went to the internet café for a bit and then back to the hotel to crash out, listening to music on my MP3 player. Our stay in Jasper was nearly at an end and the next day would see us setting off on the final leg of the rail journey overnight to Vancouver.

Thursday 14th April 2005

After another superb omelette breakfast we checked out and arranged to leave our bags in reception for a while, as the train wasn't due to leave until 3-30pm, and went for a final walk around Jasper. We didn't go far, and had the feeling that we'd done all we could, not wanting to buy any more souvenirs or drink any more beers, so ended up spending an hour or so in the internet café. With nothing else to do we both got a sandwich from Subway for the train, picked up our bags from the hotel, and walked over the road to the train station to begin the long wait for the train. By now my rucksack was too full to squeeze in the haversack at the top which I'd been doing previously, along with all the clothes and souvenirs

I'd bought, so that would have to be carried separately from now on. A bust zip also meant I needed to get a new haversack for hand luggage.

We spent over two hours inside the small Jasper station building, which was mainly spent reading but it was also a time for reflection on the journey to date and of the stay in Jasper in particular. It had been a great five days there, and in Banff, where we'd seen a good deal of what I've come to regard as the most beautiful scenery in the world. The views around Jasper, Banff, and along the Icefields Parkway in between are absolutely stunning. As I've said before, this is what we'd come to see, the image that stands out above the rest, the endless views of forested landscapes with snow capped mountains towering above.

I think we were right to base ourselves in Jasper, with its laid back feeling and pristine environment, although in hindsight we could have done more activities and less drinking, but then you can only do so much, and drinking beer does get rather tempting when on holiday! The Whistlers Inn had been a good place to stay, reasonably priced, central location, clean and spacious rooms, friendly staff, and a lively bar downstairs. It had been a great few days in the Canadian Rockies, and after the time in Jasper I knew that I wanted to go back there one day. Our attention would now turn towards Vancouver and the west coast.

As with all journeys on the VIA Rail Canadian service, the train was in long before it was due to leave and we were allowed on, but we were soon aboard and on our way out of Jasper, finding a couple of seats opposite each other, with me getting my preferred left hand side seat. I overheard a couple of other passengers talking about Jasper, saying that they liked it because it's a town in itself, a railway town, not quite so reliant on tourism as Banff, which kind of confirmed my own impression. After eating our Subway sandwiches, it was time to sit back and enjoy the scenery. To assist in my relaxation for the journey, I'd topped up a bottle of coke with the remainder of the rum from the hotel room, no point in wasting good rum after all! VIA Rail have rather strict rules against people bringing their own alcohol onto their trains, so I was a little bit alarmed at just how strong the smell of rum was as soon as I opened the bottle! Still, it did the trick and no one said anything.

In just over an hour we were over the border into British Columbia, the last Canadian province that we'd be visiting on the trip. Despite having got used to the tree covered mountainous scenery of the Rockies over the last five days, it was still nice to look at. At one point the train crew announced that we'd passed a bear on the left hand side of the train, and I think I just about got a glimpse of it, more of a blur really, so I guess I did get to see a bear after all, but can't be sure! We also passed Mount Robson, the highest mountain in the Canadian Rockies at 12,972 feet, which was quite spectacular, even though the light was fading and the view was restricted. The train crew were certainly doing a good job of keeping us informed of things, just as the crew from Toronto to Winnipeg were, but unlike the crew from Winnipeg to Jasper who we all thought were a little miserable. It soon got dark and the hours were passed by reading and listening to music, until we went down to the entertainment car to watch the evenings video, 'Alien versus Predator'. I'd seen 'Alien', I'd seen 'Predator', but not the two up against each other! Despite the poor sound quality and the noise of the train, it was quite entertaining, and after that it was time to retire for the evening. We stopped at Kamloops for what seemed a long time, and like the stop at Hornepayne on the Toronto to Winnipeg journey I couldn't sleep until we got moving again, but finally dropped off around midnight.

Chapter Six – British Columbia

Friday 15th April 2005

I managed to get a solid nights sleep and awoke just after dawn, still about an hour away from Vancouver. The skies were grey and it was pouring with rain, and with the mountains behind us I couldn't help thinking how lush the vegetation looked, obviously due to the high rainfall in this more maritime climate. It was a weird feeling as we slowly made our way through the suburbs of Vancouver, the colossal rail journey coming to an end, having crossed an entire continent from coast to coast, ocean to ocean. The train arrived on time at 7-50am, and as I stepped off the train and began walking along the platform, I filmed another short video clip on my phone, commenting "after two and half weeks, 4000 miles, 5 time zones, and God knows how many beers, we're here at the end of the line, Vancouver….and it's raining". After the relentless rain that greeted us in Halifax at the start of the journey, it seemed appropriate to be greeted with the same grey skies and persistent rainfall at the end of the line in Vancouver.

It felt strange looking at the train thinking of the 100 hours and 4000 miles that we'd travelled on them, knowing that our rail passes had fulfilled their objective and we'd not be getting on one of the VIA Rail trains again. Our hotel was the Ramada Inn on Granville Street in downtown Vancouver, so we went outside to get a taxi from the rank. The thing was, there wasn't any. And it was pouring with rain. Here we were, Friday morning rush hour in one of the largest cities in Canada, outside the main train station just after the arrival of the train from Toronto with dozens of passengers, and yet there were no taxis! Northallerton station has more taxis waiting for the 08:12 Transpennine Express from Darlington! It seemed that most other passengers had made other arrangements, as there weren't exactly many people waiting for a taxi. Finally, after trying unsuccessfully to phone one using a number found in the station, a taxi turned up and took us to the hotel, which only took about ten minutes.

Downtown Vancouver is set out in a massive grid system, rather like Manhattan, so it looked quite easy to navigate our way around. Our hotel was at the opposite end of Granville Street from the main downtown area, and to be honest the area looked a little bit seedy and scruffy, which was certainly in contrast to the pleasant surroundings of Jasper. The hotel was nice and clean inside though, the room was small but clean, and the view from the window was amazing. We could see at least 6 feet into the distance where an attractive red brick wall greeted us! It made the room a little dull especially with the grey skies, but it was good to be able to dump off our stuff, get showered and changed, ready to explore the delights of Vancouver. The plan for the weekend was to spend the day walking around downtown Vancouver, have a few drinks later on, go for a meal in Chinatown to compare to the one in London's Chinatown three weeks earlier, then go over to Victoria by floatplane on the Saturday, back for a final night out in Vancouver, before flying back to England on Sunday evening.

As with in Halifax, we weren't going to let the rain stop our sightseeing plans, so after a reasonably priced and satisfying breakfast in a nearby Chinese café, we walked down Granville Street heading for the far end near the waterfront. As with most of the other cities we'd been to, we soon found an indoor shopping mall with the obligatory Sears and The Bay department stores, where we both bought yet more clothes to stuff into our bags. I'd heard before going and had seen plenty of leaflets since arriving that you can claim back the sales tax in Canada on goods and services purchased, so was making sure that I as keeping the receipts of everything I was buying, as they had to be stamped by customs when leaving the country and then sent off with the appropriate form. Accommodation wasn't included, but hotel services such as laundry, as well as the clothes and souvenirs counted towards the tax refund.

The good thing about downtown Vancouver is that it's all fairly compact, and the grid system makes it fairly easy to find your way around, so it's ideal for walking. Once we were bored of shopping we went up the Vancouver Lookout Tower located on West Hastings Street, at the end of Seymour Street near the harbour area, which is kind of like a mini-CN Tower. The tower, located on top of the Harbour Centre building, is 581 feet high, making it the third highest building in Canada, and the viewing deck offers a fantastic 360 degrees unobstructed view of Vancouver. Although it was overcast and raining which limited the view somewhat, we still had a great view of the city and surrounding area. Whilst taking enough photos to get a full 360 degrees view of Vancouver, we recognised quite a few of the sights, seeing right down to the area where our hotel was, the ice hockey arena, Chinatown, the huge docks area with all the container freight, Canada Place, and also quite a few float planes taking off and landing.

We were unsure of what to do next so we spent quite some time up there taking in the view, before getting a coffee and reading through some tourist leaflets. There weren't many people up there so it was quite chilled out, and after much indecision we decided that we'd go to the IMAX cinema at Canada Place, which is a large convention and exhibition centre sticking out into the harbour on a massive pier. The lift in the tower is nothing compared to the CN Tower in Toronto, but it's still on the outside of the building and it still ascends and descends quite some height in not much time, and it's great watching the surrounding buildings and the ground get closer and closer as you go down, or vice versa. It was still raining outside but we took our time getting to Canada Place, taking in views of the docks and of the float planes on the way.

The exhibition centre is huge, and there must have been various conferences going on given the amount of people around, many looking dressed for the occasion. We were told that the IMAX cinema is right down at the far end of the complex, which took a few minutes to walk down to. The IMAX cinema is basically a huge 3D cinematic experience, where you're given some delightfully large plastic glasses which enable you to see the image on screen clearly and in 3D. There were two films on show when we were there, one was an African safari, and the other was about various marine life, both being about 45 minutes long, and seeing as we had plenty of time we decided to watch both.

After a short wait we took our seats for the African safari, which turned out to be in South Africa. I was slightly surprised but it really was a fantastic experience, very well made. The film is taken mostly from the back of a safari jeep, with a rather attractive young lady turning round and talking to the camera, and it almost feels as if you're actually sat in the jeep with her. Various park guides also join in on the safari and add their knowledge to enhance the experience, and the background music added to the occasion even more, much of it being a version of the South African national anthem. All this made me think of my many South African cousins, living both in England and South Africa, and how much I want to go there someday. All in all an excellent film, with the filming, 3D effects and sound combining to make it feel almost like you're actually there.

Given my experience of scuba diving, including the shark and dolphin dives at Port Lucaya, Grand Bahama Island, I was looking forward to the marine life film slightly more than the safari one. There was some fantastic filming on screen, especially with the camera going through huge shoals of fish which looked spectacular in 3D, and there was some good images of sharks, but I couldn't help feeling a little disappointed by this one, mainly I think because it was difficult to get any reference for the scale of the marine life. The scenes were changing that much and inconsistently that it was a bit difficult to follow, due to the absence of any divers for scale or of the sea bed and surface to gauge the depth. What would have been good would have been a small series of dives presented in the same style as the African safari. Still quite enjoyable though.

Once we'd finished up there we went back outside to find it still raining, and made our way back to the hotel, which was only about 20 minutes walk. After changing into some newly acquired clobber it was time to hit the town, and our first stop was Doolins pub on Granville Street, just a few hundred yards back towards the main downtown area. This was an Irish pub on the corner, quite a decent and popular place, and we sat at the bar to enjoy the first beers of the night. It was funny being sat at the bar getting text messages from some mates back home at the end of their night, with it being 2am back in England, but 6pm in Vancouver and our night just beginning. After Doolins it was back across the road to Speak Easy, a trendy type bar which was still fairly quiet, so we had another couple in there sat at the bar, before moving on towards Chinatown. As we got nearer to Chinatown we found a pub called Churchills, which was quite a large, dark traditional drinkers pub, we had one in there before hunger told us to get to Chinatown quickly and get some food!

We had no idea what Chinatown would be like and only a rough idea of where it was, but we didn't expect it to be very much like London's Chinatown, which is right in the middle of the West End and very much caters for tourists. As we reached Vancouver's Chinatown we realised just how different it was. On one hand it was nice to appreciate a genuine Chinatown without all of the artificiality of the one in London, but on the other hand I couldn't help thinking how run down it all looked. The streets were very quiet, all signs were in Chinese, there were no pubs or what you might call usual shops, just restaurants and Chinese food shops. It really did feel off the beaten track so to speak, and it was almost a touch worrying to see the only people around were congregated in groups on street corners. We selected a random restaurant, in which everyone else was Chinese, and ordered some food. I have to say I enjoyed the tea that they give out for free, most refreshing. As for the meal I just ordered chicken fried rice which was a bit bland on it's own. Very filling as well, and once I'd cleared my plate I began to wonder if was such a good idea to eat all the rice on top of all that beer when there was much more beer to come!

Once we left we headed back to normal Vancouver, i.e. where there's bars, and first stop was at a place called Malones, on the corner of Seymour Street and West Pender street. This was one of the usual North American bar grill type places, but quite a decent place. After all that rice we were too bloated to drink beer, so it was time to hit the spirits already! I started off on rum and coke, Chris had vodka and coke, which became doubles, and given the larger measures over there the drink soon started to perk us up after the lethargic after effects of eating too much. After there we headed down Granville Street towards the hotel, stopping in a bar called Lennox. In here we had a mixture of rum / vodka and coke, before progressing onto cocktails, which went down a treat. Next stop was Morrisseys pub adjacent to our hotel, and in here we got chatting to a couple of nice women from Seattle, with whom we went for another drink in Doolins where I went back on the beer for some reason. After beer, rice, rum, coke, cocktails and more beer, I was running out of drinks and I was struggling, not too drunk but just couldn't stomach much more drink, so we left the Seattle ladies and returned to the hotel to crash out for the night.

Saturday 16th April 2005

Saturday 16 April and it was our last full day in Canada. The 3 weeks since leaving Northallerton had flown by, and our last major outing of the holiday was the trip to Victoria. We got a taxi from the hotel up to the Sea Plane Terminal, missing breakfast due to feeling a touch rough from the night before, and once we'd checked in and paid we sat around for nearly an hour due to arriving so early, having thought it better to get up and get there early to save rushing. It was the first time for both of us on a float plane, and it was sure to be a good experience. After a while most of the other passengers arrived, and it was time to get on board the DeHavilland Twin Otter 18 seater. It looked quite small from the outside, and sure enough it was small and cramped inside, but the flight was only 35 minutes. It would certainly be an experience. The plane has an engine on each wing (which is why it's called a 'Twin' Otter!), and was certainly noisy and you could feel the power as the thrust was increased to get us moving. It felt weird powering along the water, a little daunting as well, but once up in the air I felt far more relaxed than I do in a larger aircraft. As the pilot pointed out, although there are lifejackets under the seats, we wouldn't need them as we were mostly flying over water and we were in a float plane!

The flight took us right over downtown Vancouver, and then directly over VCR, Vancouver International Airport, before we got over the sea. I'd actually done part of the flight on Microsoft Flight Simulator so had some idea of what it would be like! Seeing Vancouver disappear to the left to see Vancouver Island approach to the right was quite spectacular. As a guess I'd say that we were flying at around 8,000 feet, and it was great seeing the coastline unfold as we got nearer to Victoria. Luckily I had a window seat so was able to appreciate the view a bit more, and we were only two rows from the front so could see into the small cockpit to keep an eye on the two pilots. The descent was very gentle and the landing, although making me a little apprehensive, was actually a lot smoother than I thought it would be, and we were soon sailing across the harbour to the sea plane terminal. All in all it was a very enjoyable experience.

We had about six hours to see Victoria, which is more than we had in Ottawa, and the only plan was to walk around the harbour and surrounding area, check out a few shops, and most importantly go on one of the whale watching trips. As we walked up from the sea plane terminal and quayside area we reached a large tourist shop, outside which a delightfully stunning blonde lady was selling the whale watching tours. It didn't take us much persuading to book onto the afternoon trip with them, which would be leaving at 2-30pm and take about 2 hours. I was a little concerned as we were supposed to check in for our flight by 4-30pm, but she checked with West Coast Air who they work with just to let them know that we'd be on the whale watching trip and may be a few minutes late, and there was no problem with that. We'd basically be going out on a large dinghy, and would have to wear these delightful looking orange survival suits as a precaution, in the hope of seeing some killer whales, or orcas to give them their proper name. In contrast to Vancouver the weather in Victoria was nice and sunny, and she advised us to wear sunglasses due to the glare off the water. Neither of us anticipated that when we left the hotel so would have to buy some more.

With over two hours to kill before returning to the delightful sales assistant to get ready for the trip out to sea, we went into a café across the road for some breakfast / lunch. After a sandwich, coffee and sickly chocolate cookie in there, we walked around a few blocks before going into the shopping mall and finding the usual Bay store in there. Both of us bought a cap and sunglasses, then sat around and chilled out for a while in the mall. I made a quick phone call home to my mum, just to say we were having a whale of a time (sorry, couldn't resist it!) and were going whale watching. We then went back down to the very picturesque harbour area, and just took in the sights and sounds, watching a very skilful and charismatic entertainer juggling with fire whilst on a nine foot high unicycle! It was good stood there watching the entertainment, and he was certainly keeping the crowd amused. I was gradually feeling worse and worse though, with growing feelings of nausea. Obviously mixing all those drinks on top of the Chinese the night before was beginning to play havoc with my stomach, and it got to the point where I was looking around for somewhere that would have a toilet just in case I needed to be sick.

Once the juggler had finished I suggested we walked along in front of the British Columbia Parliament building (Victoria is the capital of BC), which has a delightful statue of Queen Victoria in front of it, where I took some pictures before we headed for a bar up the road. My stomach was really feeling bad now, and I knew that only being sick would cure it, so as we went in I told Chris to get me a lemonade. Now those that know me, how many times have you seen me go into a pub and order a lemonade?! There was no way I could handle a beer though, and the lemonade would help to settle my stomach. So having reached the safety of a toilet I let my stomach do what it wanted to do and was reintroduced with the sandwich, cookie and coffee from the café. I felt slightly better anyway, and then sat and enjoyed a nice lemonade! I have to say that I was wondering if going out on the sea in a dinghy after throwing up was such a good idea, but I was determined not to miss out on the whale watching.

At around 2pm we made our way around to the other side of the marina to the whale watching kiosk where we'd been earlier, and waited for our call to get ready. It was getting quite warm by now, which would make the trip out to see a bit more pleasant. There were six other people who turned up for the trip, and first of all we had to put our bright orange survival suits on. Given the increasing heat it was certainly warm inside the suits, so I left my jacket with the lovely sales assistant and off we all went, walking across the road and down to the marina in our bright orange suits. It felt good to get going after all the waiting around, and although my stomach wasn't 100% I was feeling a bit better. After a briefing from the skipper of the boat we were on our way. We would be leaving the harbour and travelling out around the coast to where some killer whales we known to have been sighted earlier that day. He told us that killer whales, or orcas to give them their proper name, aren't actually whales at all but are large porpoises. The orcas we'd be seeing were the transient orcas who hunt small mammals such as seals. Hmm, what about humans who fall out of boats?!

Once out of the harbour we speeded up considerably, and against expectation the effect of bouncing along over the waves totally settled my stomach, so as well as being very exhilarating in itself the motion was making feel so much better. I've always enjoyed being out at sea, whether on a ferry or on a dive boat, and being out on the large dinghy, at the end of the great three week trans-Canadian adventure, out at sea on what was practically the Pacific Ocean, at the furthest point west I've ever been, gave me a great sense of satisfaction and a feeling of well being. There's something soothing about being at sea, whilst at the same time it gives a feeling of adventure and excitement. After a few miles or soaring across the water, with the occasional soaking from the waves, we stopped for a couple of minutes near a small bay to observes some seals, and then headed out to a place called Race Rocks.

This is basically like a small mountain sticking out of the deep water of the Straits of Juan de Fuca, which separates Canada from the USA (Washington State), with strong and deep currents sweeping into the rocks. The rocks are located one nautical mile (1.15 miles) from Rocky Point, the southernmost point on Vancouver Island, 12 nautical miles (13.8 miles) from Victoria and 12 nautical miles from the American shore. A lighthouse was built on the rocks in 1860, situated on the 'Great Rock' which is no more than a hundred yards across and fairly flat along the top, and other than that they are home to a large number of sea lions and birds, who prefer the smaller undeveloped rocks. These sea lions apparently travel up from the coast of California and Mexico, and are part of the reason why the transient orcas are in the area. The darkness of the blue water gave some indication of the depth here, which despite being so close to shore was up to 500 feet deep in places.

As we were watching the sea lions the skipper got a call from another boat to say that they had seen some orcas a couple of miles away, so we quickly headed further west to see the stars of the show. The engines were cut and then we waited to catch a glimpse of the orcas, and whilst doing so we were told that they spend about 30 seconds on three or four short dives followed by longer dives of 5-10 minutes. It was quite fun scanning the water trying to get glimpse of one of the whales, and finally we saw two of them a few hundred yards away, first their dorsal fins and then their tail fins as they dived down. I managed to get a couple of pictures, but with me just having a 35mm compact camera with 28mm wide angle lens, they weren't much more than little specs near the horizon! Still, we'd seen what we'd come out on the boat to see, and we spent the next half hour or so moving around to various location to get another look at the two transient orcas who were on the hunt for some tasty seals.

Eventually it was time to head back to Victoria, with a feeling of satisfaction having seen a couple of killer whales / transient orcas, and a feeling of relief that the trip out on the boat had actually settled my stomach after the earlier upset. All in all it seemed like a great end to the trip, we'd gone as far west as we could by train then went further west by plane and boat. We were soon back into the harbour, and getting off the boat and walking back up to the shop in our survival suits made us feel like astronauts getting off the space shuttle or something! It certainly felt good to replace that suit with my jacket. Once changed we were straight over to the sea plane terminal to check in for our flight back to Vancouver, and after a short wait we were on our way again, although this time I felt much more relaxed as we sped along the water and took off into the air. The skies by now had become even clearer, and we had great views looking across to Washington State and the southern approach to Vancouver. Surprisingly it had even stopped raining in Vancouver, so once we'd landed we had a leisurely stroll back down Granville Street towards the hotel.

The shops were closing and the people weren't out for the night yet, so it was quite a peaceful walk and also nice not to be dodging the rain drops. Having not eaten all afternoon (and in my case what I'd eaten previously no longer being where it should have been!) we decided to stop off on the way back for something to eat, choosing to go into Torchys bar quite near the hotel. This was a small bar / grill establishment, quite similar to the Speak Easy bar we'd been in the night before, with not many other people in but there was another stunning barmaid. I felt ready for more beer, so had a couple of bottles of Moose beer, and chose 'BC halibut and chips' for the meal. When it finally arrived the halibut, a type of fish I was trying for the first time, was beautiful, strong tasting, absolutely delicious. The 'chips' though were horrible, those skinny little fries that have so much salt they must be cooked in sea water! I'm not a big fan of salt, so needless to say I left most of the so called 'chips', but thoroughly enjoyed the fish.

By now it was around 7pm, and the plan was to crash out in the hotel for a bit, freshen up and then go out for a few beers, with it being the last night in Canada. I'd sent a text to Jessica from Seattle who we'd been talking to the night before, but got no reply, and once back at the hotel we both crashed out and were that knackered neither of us could be bothered to go out, so that was that, no more beer in Canada. Thoughts now would turn to the trip home, and I usually find that on the last day of a holiday, with the waiting at the airport and the long flight ahead of us, all I want to do is get home, stick my feet up, watch Sky Sports News, and have a proper cup of tea.

Chapter Seven – Homeward Bound

Sunday 17th April 2005

At 6am Rogers Sportsnet were showing live coverage of Newcastle United v Manchester United in the FA Cup Semi-Final, so I set my alarm for that. That really reinforced the time difference of 8 hours, there was me in bed at 6am Pacific Daylight Time watching football back home where it was 2pm British Summer Time. I was hoping for Newcastle to win but true to form Man U stuffed them 4-0. Oh well, time for breakfast and we went next door to the Morrisseys pub which cooked breakfasts for guests of the hotel, our last North American style breakfast with poor quality bacon and too many hash browns, served with weak tea.

Even though the flight back home wasn't leaving until 6pm, we couldn't think of anything to do so got a taxi from the hotel down to the airport at about 11am. Vancouver International Airport is about 8 miles from the city centre, and for once we had quite a talkative taxi driver who was a good laugh. We checked in straight away to get rid of our heavy new clothes and souvenir filled rucksacks, through customs to the departure gate area, ready for a very long wait. It was at this point that I realised I'd forgotten to get all my receipts stamped to claim the sales tax back on the clothes I'd bought, and I found out that I should have done this before checking in. B*gger! Not happy! So with nothing else to do, we spent the next few hours sat by the window of the terminal, looking out at the planes, reading books and magazines, drinking coffee and discussing the highlights of the trip.

Finally, after a change of departure gate, it was time to board and we were on our way. Or so we thought. Our seats were down near the back of the plane, I had a window seat again, but right in front of us was a family with four young children including a screaming baby. The baby was proper doing my head in, I mean, babies have every right to scream but surely parents shouldn't take kids so young on a plane. To their credit all the other kids were quiet and well behaved. However, just as we started taxiing towards the runway, we stopped for about twenty minutes, and then the over the PA system came the announcement "Ladies and Gentlemen, er… this is your captain speaking, we've err, been undergoing some tests and the engineers have found a problem with the aircraft, so just as a err precaution, we're going to have to return to the terminal so the problem can be investigated." "That's bloody marvellous" I thought (or words to that effect!). I wanted to get off that plane, a screaming kid in front of me, the plane having problems, and that after Chris told me to stop whistling 'Leaving on a jet plane' when we left the hotel as John Denver who sung it died in a plane crash and it might be a bad luck omen.

Despite my frustration at the situation I put on the classical music and carried on reading my book. What else could I do? Finally, after nearly an hour back at the terminal we were on our way, and this time got all the way to the runway and were cleared for take off. I have to say I was more paranoid than ever about the take off, and had visions of engine failure as we got into the air, but we were soon up in the air and I was feeling relieved. The engine noise and the headphones almost blanked out the sound of the screaming baby, and I was able to enjoy some good views of the Rocky Mountains before it got dark. It seemed strange flying over the second largest country in the world in a matter of hours, having spent three weeks crossing by land. We took a more northerly route though as it's obviously more direct than sticking to the same latitude, and I managed to get about half an hour sleep before waking up to bright sunshine.

Monday 18th April 2005

It's always fascinating to see recognisable land from the air, and we came down over the Outer Hebrides, west coast of Scotland, the Lake District and Wales, before going into a holding pattern over Berkshire and Hampshire for about 20 minutes. It's quite eerie sometimes looking out and seeing all the other planes stacked up in the sky, waiting to land, thinking that we're just a small number on a screen somewhere, with people making sure the small number goes nowhere near other numbers on the screen. We eventually landed safe and sound, into the delights of a bustling Heathrow Airport with it's multinational crowds, went through customs, got our bags and walked to the Underground station. I didn't have any change on me so couldn't use the ticket machines, the change machine was out of order and the queue for the ticket kiosk was being held up by confused Australian travellers asking how much it is to every station in London. When I finally got to the front of the queue I was served by an obnoxious, rude and miserable person with a limited command of English who practically threw the ticket onto the counter without a smile or word of thanks. Needless to say after walking half a mile with my bags, feeling hot, not happy at the delays and the service, and suffering from jet lag, I made my feelings known as I walked off and then got onto the train. But then I just sat and laughed as I said to Chris "five minutes back in the rat race and I'm already p***ed off"! It was so great to be back in England!

After an hour on the tube followed by two and a half hours on the train, during which we were both struggling to keep awake due to the lack of sleep, we arrived back into Northallerton. It seemed strange to be on a train without the cards above our seats with the destination scribbled on. Without the 18 inches of legroom. Without the foot rest. Without the frozen landscape of Nova Scotia. Without the brightly painted houses of Quebec. Without the rolling tree-covered hills and bare rocks of western Ontario. Without the endless plains of Alberta. Without the observation car providing dramatic views of towering Rocky Mountains. Without the video and games car providing entertainment. Without the cans of Labatts Blue which had to be drunk at one's seat. Without the bilingual announcements. Without the constant feeling of adventure as we headed further and further west. Instead we had a more crowded yet more modern GNER train, with flat farmland, small market towns, larger industrial towns, and finally the sight of the North Yorkshire Moors to greet us, meaning it was back to Northallerton, back to everyday life. But first I had that cup of tea to drink, with my feet up, watching Sky Sports News, feeling content after the amazing trip I'd just completed, before sleeping off the jet lag.

The whole trip had been an amazing experience. I had been to somewhere I had wanted to go for so long. I had completed an epic journey over such an amazing and diverse country. Everything had gone to plan as far as travel arrangement were concerned. As for the highlights? Well Halifax seemed a special kind of place. I know it was cold and wet when we were there, but I liked the feel of it. It had an almost homely feel to it. I would definitely like to go back there again, and also to explore more of Nova Scotia. Toronto had been good with it being a base for various other trips, and as a city it feels quite clean and safe. Jasper was amazing and it's somewhere I would love to go back to. It presented the image that I described at the beginning of this book, the one that stands out above the rest, the one of dramatic, stunning, mountainous scenery, with immense forests interspersed with lakes, an image of pure beauty and freedom. And finally Victoria as well was a highlight, despite our visit being only a few hours, with its attractive inner harbour and the exhilarating boat trip.

Canadians themselves are great people. They seem to have the best of both British and Americans without the worst of both. Polite, friendly and intelligent is one way of describing them. As for the next trip to Canada, Nova Scotia, Toronto, Jasper and Victoria all deserve another visit for the reasons outlined above. I'd also like to see Edmonton and Calgary which we missed out on this trip. I'd like to spend some time in Newfoundland. And I'd like to take a trip up north someday, both to Churchill on the edge of the Hudson Bay, and to places like Dawson and Yellowknife up in the Yukon and North West Territories.

Probably my biggest regret about the trip was my choice of camera. I'd toyed with the idea of buying my first digital camera before the trip, but decided not to bother and instead took a Nikon 35mm compact with 28mm wide angle lens. Great camera as far a 35mm cameras are concerned, and I took four 36 exposure films of good quality prints, capturing some of my favourite memories of the trip from east to west. However, when I purchased a digital camera a couple of months after the trip I was astounded at the clarity of the images, especially with those I took on a trip to Norway in August. I'd not been too bothered about a digital camera for years, but once purchased I was so glad I'd made the transition. The camera I went for was the Pentax Optio 5s, which is a great little camera. The ease of use, the size of the camera, the additional facilities such as video clips, the picture quality, the number of pictures that can be stored, being able to delete unwanted or stored pictures, all add up to make digital cameras a far better option.

As for the ice hockey, a deal finally got resolved to ensure an NHL season could be played for 2005-06. Alas the Toronto Maple Leafs failed to make the post season play-offs in April 2006, but I did at least get to see them play. I'd been hoping to meet up with my friends Mel and Sue on their world tour at some point along the way, and with them spending New Year in New York this was always the most likely option. So me and a couple of friends from Northallerton, Daz and Chi, flew out in late December to JFK, met Mel and Sue just off Times Square, and spent a memorable five days there including a short trip into New Jersey to see the Leafs beat New Jersey Devils 6-3 on New Year's Eve. A fantastic trip to end a year of fantastic travelling experiences, with a five day trip to Norway in August adding to the three weeks in Canada. My thoughts soon turned to the next big trip.

Having enjoyed the trans-Canadian rail trip so much, and having a lifetime ambition to visit every continent on Earth, the trans-Siberian express via Mongolia looks like a very good option, which would enable me to see a fair bit of Asia, travelling from Moscow to Beijing in two weeks . South America also interests me, mainly Chile and southern Argentina, but the lack of a decent rail network means that would involve planes and buses rather than trains. But then as the first anniversary of the Canada trip arrived, the option of going to Canada again seemed all the more appealing, but this time going west to east and this time driving across the country.

The idea of a road trip seemed like the number one option, as it would be a different experience, allow us more flexibility and allow us to see more remote places other than Jasper. The cost of hiring a car, collecting in Vancouver and dropping off in Halifax I calculated to be about £500 plus petrol. On the other hand, doing the train trip in reverse also seemed appealing, mainly as it cut out the hassle of driving, and meant we weren't guessing at travelling times, instead having the certainly of the train timetables. Either way it seemed like a great idea, but as is often the case when planning trips away, an initial expression of interest from someone peters away to a lack of interest or the "can't afford it" excuse. So with the three or four others interested all dropping out of a big trip in Autumn 2006, I ended up going on a one week trip to Toronto with Chris.

I found an excellent deal on this over the internet, the flight with Air Transat and six nights in the 3 star Days Hotel in downtown Toronto for the amazing price of £342. During the big trans-Canadian trip of 2005 we used Toronto as a base for five days but never saw an awful lot of the city, and due to the NHL lockout we never got to see the Toronto Maple Leafs, so this trip was the chance to address that. In the six days over there in November 2006 we saw a much larger area of downtown, with the hotel being up on College Street just off Yonge Street.

We visited the nearby Duke of Gloucester British pub and the Hoops sports bar (with about a hundred TV screens!) on most days, lured by the peculiar feel of being at a 'local' pub with the former and by the endless sports coverage, including English football, in the latter. We saw the Leafs beat the New York Islanders 4-2, a great experience to be there after watching so many live games on TV at midnight back home. We visited Historic Fort York, founded in 1793 when York (renamed Toronto in 1834) was first established, and learnt a bit more about the area's history, in particular the War of 1812 with the USA (being able to hold a musket and 'fix bayonet' was a particular highlight for me, especially after all the Sharpe novels and history books I've read on that era!). We went to the Hockey Hall of Fame on Yonge Street, a museum dedicated to Canada's national sport where the Stanley Cup can be seen. I had fun with the shooting practice there, where you get to shook pucks at a virtual reality goalie, although like many others I scored 0/5!

We went up the CN Tower on a calm and clear day (unlike last time), this time going to the upper observation desk at 1465 feet, getting some amazing views and subsequent photos. It felt strangely calming to be sat drinking tea in the café on the main observation deck, looking down over the city, seeing the grid system of the downtown area and the skyscrapers of the business district laid out below us. And on the final day there, we took a helicopter flight over the downtown area from Toronto City Centre Airport, only 8 minutes long and costing about $90CAN, but a truly memorable and worthwhile experience.

The extra week in Toronto in a way complimented the trans-Canadian trip of the year before, being able to see one of the places visited in much more detail, although it did feel strange not going anywhere else by train, like a 31 hour journey to Winnipeg. To add to what I'd said after the first visit, I maintain that Toronto is a great city, but it's slight more congested and slightly run down than I thought previously. The place is absolutely huge, and at least this time I was able to appreciate the size of the city a little more. As far as big cities go (I prefer rural areas having lived most of my life in villages or small towns), it's a great place, low crime, lots to do, very cosmopolitan, and I expect to visit again someday, probably to see both the Leafs and the newly formed Toronto FC who have joined the Major Soccer League from 2007. The things that struck me in particular were the amount of homeless people, the amount of food establishments (can no one there cook?!), and that despite the large number of different ethnic backgrounds and Canada's positively multi-cultural policies, everyone was basically Canadian first regardless of their background.

All in it was all another excellent trip to a fantastic country. Thoughts would now finally turn to the next 'big trip', and with my brother Dan expressing an interest in going to Canada and the USA, the idea of doing another trans-Canadian rail trip began to take hold in the Spring of 2007. I'd considered doing the trans-Siberian rail trip, which seems an excellent way of travelling across Asia and seeing the far east, but with memories of the 2005 trip, sporting interests, and ease of travel, the lure of Canada became too much and so this became the choice of destination for Off The Rails Part Two.

Niagara Falls, Ontario, 4th April 2005

Houses of Parliament, Ottawa, Ontario, 1st April 2005

Pyramid Lake, Jasper, Alberta, 12th April 2005

Victoria, British Columbia, 16th April 2005

Steam Clock, Vancouver, British Columbia, 21st September 2007

Whistlers Inn, Jasper, Alberta, 24th September 2007

Toronto, Ontario, 4th October 2007

Manhattan, New York, 6th October 2007

Part Two – From West to East - Autumn 2007

The trans-Canadian rail trip of 2005 that you have just been reading about had been a truly amazing and unique journey that both fulfilled a dream and inspired future ambitions. To me, long distance rail travel is a much better way of seeing a far off land, both with the journey itself and the stops along the way. It makes the viewing of a world map so much more rewarding when one can point and say "I've travelled across there over three weeks" rather than "I flew over there in six hours". In a plane, you can be anywhere in the world. It's the same seating, the same food, the same mix of passengers, the same cabin crew, the same clouds, the same sea, the same land. Obviously there are variations within that, but what I'm trying to get across is that flying is just a quick and convenient way to get *to* somewhere, it's not really travelling *across* somewhere.

With long distance rail journeys though, you get the different styles of trains which reflect the countries they travel through (that's the full extent of my train spotting credentials!). You get to see ever changing landscapes unfold minute by minute (with obvious exceptions such as Saskatchewan by night!) from a level and perspective where you can appreciate what you're seeing, whether it's dramatic forest covered mountains, rolling hills, open farmland, small villages or large cities. You see and hear a wider cross-section of fellow passengers, from tourists travelling long distance to local workers travelling just a few stops. You get the time to think about the journey, all that you've seen and expect to see, and the time to put it all in context. And then of course you have the joy of all the stops along the way, a few days to get a real feel for the land you're travelling across, to experience local culture, see the landscape, feel the climatic differences, and of course taste the local culinary and alcoholic delights!

So, with the idea of doing the trans-Canadian in reverse taking hold, with the plan being to travel in the autumn of 2007, and again taking about three weeks, I began to turn my attention towards the route to be taken. Travelling west to east across Canada would mean starting in Vancouver, so flying to there would be the first leg of the journey. Beyond that I had a number of ideas. One was to head north from Winnipeg up to Churchill on the edge of the Hudson Bay. As I've mentioned before when considering the route for the 2005 trip, this would take up six days of the journey, involving a 36 hour train journey up there, with the train back leaving three and a half days later (unless one opted for the taking the same train back to Winnipeg 12 hours after arriving, which would be pretty pointless). The thought of seeing the northern lights, polar bears waiting for the ice to reform across the Hudson Bay, and travelling across a sub-arctic landscape did seem quite appealing, but the six days would limit the time available for elsewhere.

The two definite destinations were Jasper and Toronto. Jasper, in the heart of the Canadian Rockies, is an amazing place, one which typifies the vision of Canada. One thing that that will live with me forever is the amazement of the scenery after disembarking from the train in Jasper, looking around, taking in the natural beauty, and saying the one word which seemed to sum it all up – "wow"! So spending a few days in Jasper was a must for the second trip, this time perhaps hiring a car one day and a bike another day, and seeing what other organised trips would be available. Spending the required extra days in Jasper limited the time that could be spent stopping elsewhere, and I decided that as much as I wanted to see places I'd not visited before such as Edmonton, the extra time in Jasper would take precedence over spending a couple of days in another large North American city.

Although by 2007 I'd been to Toronto twice, I'd enjoyed both visits, it's a natural break in the journey, and that's where my sporting interests lie. In addition to the Toronto Maple Leafs NHL team, as I've mentioned in the previous chapter, from 2007 Toronto has its own football team playing in North America's MLS (Major League Soccer), playing in a new purpose build stadium called the BMO Field (which strangely enough for Toronto has virtually no roofs over the stands). Ideally, I wanted to be in Toronto on a day when both Toronto FC and the Leafs would be playing at home, which given that the NHL season doesn't start until early October, and the MLS season ends in late October, limits the times when that would happen.

Beyond Toronto I became focused on two main options. One was to return where it all began in March 2005, Halifax, Nova Scotia, via Quebec City. This would give me the chance to see Quebec, visiting the site of the battle in 1759 when British troops scaled the cliffs from the St Lawrence river and defeated the French within 20 minutes, and also give me the chance to practise my French language skills. Furthermore, it would give me the chance to see more of Nova Scotia, with the plan of hiring a car from Halifax one day and going for a long drive, and in a way having Halifax as the end of the trip would be quite symbolic, as I say having started the 2005 trip from there.

The other option would be to take the train to New York, stopping at Niagara Falls along the way, and experiencing the delights of the city where I started 2006, before flying back from there. Although not Canada, this would still complete a remarkable North American coast to coast rail trip, and although the VIA Rail pass can't be used in the USA, the price of a regular ticket from Niagara to New York is less than £50. The other option would be to get a return to New York and still take in Quebec and Nova Scotia, although this would obviously reduce the time available to spend in these places.

With my oldest brother Dan being the only other person expressing a serious interest in going, I had to give consideration to his preferences for a route, and as he'd not been to New York before this was quite understandably going to be the preferred option. To add something new for myself, I looked at options for north east USA and decided that Boston would be a great place to visit, quite historical as far as American history goes, and I'd heard that the train journey from New York to Boston was quite spectacular as it follows the coast northwards. So, by June 2007 we'd agreed on the route, this being Vancouver to Jasper to Toronto to New York to Boston, and just had to wait for the NHL fixtures (or schedule as they say in North America) to be published in July.

I found a great flight with KLM which would fly from Teesside Airport (or Durham Tees Valley as they call it now, stupid name if you ask me, it's nowhere near the city of Durham, Darlington yes, it's in the Tees Valley, it's in County Durham, but miles from the city of Durham!), just 15 miles from where I live and 3 miles from where my other brother Barney lives. This would involve a flight to Amsterdam where I would meet Dan (flying in from Stavanger), then we'd get the afternoon flight to Vancouver, and do the same in reverse from Boston. This would save the hassle of getting the train down to London as I normally do for trans-Atlantic trips, although it would seem weird flying east to go west.

On Wednesday 11th July, the NHL schedule was published, as expected the Leafs were at home to Ottawa on the first night of the season, Wednesday 3rd October, so all the plans fell into place, flying out to Vancouver on Thursday 20th September and back into Teesside Darlington Durham Tees Valley International Airport on Saturday 13th October, just in time to watch England v Estonia in the afternoon. By the weekend, the flights with KLM were booked, we had hotel rooms reserved in Vancouver, Jasper, Toronto, New York and Boston, the rail passes were reserved, I'd bought tickets for the Toronto FC match, and just had to wait for tickets to become available for the Maple Leafs game.

It was a relief that the countdown could finally begin to the trans-North American experience part two, and all that remained was to work a bit more overtime and save a bit more money, and to get those Leafs tickets of course. In the end I bought some tickets for the Leafs v Sens game form on online ticket agent, above face value (US$420 for 2 tickets including $50 Fed-Ex delivery, so about £100 each!) but at least we'd have tickets guaranteed, although due to late availability and subsequent despatch I had to arrange to have the tickets delivered to the hotel I'd booked in Toronto, after checking with the hotel by e-mail. So, with that all sorted, it was finally time for part 2 of the big trans-North American adventure!

Chapter 1 – British Columbia

Thursday 20th September 2007

With a 6am flight from Teesside to Amsterdam, and a similar start for Dan flying from Stavanger to Amsterdam, it would be an early start to the trip and a very long day, given that we'd be arriving in Vancouver at 4-15pm local time, 12-15am UK time. I had one dilemma in the morning though – should I take my waterproof Berghaus jacket as well as my Aquascutum jacket (different from the last trip but similar design)? I'd changed my mind about three times the night before, due to the space available, wanting to keep plenty of room for things I'd buy, and in the end decided not to bother – as in 2005 when I decided against taking secondary footwear at the last minute, I'd end up regretting that decision!

I was up at 3am, away at 3-50am to my parents, and got to the airport just after 4-30am, where my dad would drive my car back from and pick me up three weeks later. For someone who often makes the most of the flexibility of the flexi-time system at work, it's amazing how easy it was to get up and about so early. I'd checked in online, a new experience for me, so just had to check the baggage in, straight through to Vancouver so I wouldn't have to collect it at Amsterdam, then sat around until the flight was called. This ended up being late, but we were on board and ready to go not long after 6am, or so I thought. After what seemed ages of being sat on the plane without even the engines starting, the captain announced that there was a problem with the pitot indicator heater or something which measures the airspeed, and this would be liable to freezing over depending on the weather, so we had to sit and wait for weather reports from Amsterdam. Rather frustrating and a touch worrying, but at least I had plenty of time for the connecting flight from Amsterdam which wasn't due to leave until 3-30pm (Dutch time). Eventually the captain announced that we'd fly at low altitude to avoid the pitot indicator freezing, so at about 7-15am we were finally on our way, after I sent an SMS to Dan informing him of the late arrival of my flight.

The announcement that the flight would only take 55 minutes was a bonus, half an hour shorter than expected, and it was quite interesting flying at a lower level, generally keeping below 10,000 feet, especially as Teesside to Amsterdam is another flight I've done on the Microsoft flight simulator. After being served a light breakfast we began our descent and went into clouds at around 6,000 feet, and were at only few hundred feet and on final approach when we finally broke through the clouds. Once landed we spent about 10 minutes taxiing to the terminal, on what was my first time at Schiphol Airport and it really is huge. A bus took us from the plane to the terminal itself, and I soon met up with Dan near one of the bars, leaving us some 5 hours until the boarding of our flight to Vancouver.

The time was spent wandering around, eating and drinking, although with us flying we didn't drink too much alcohol. It was quite good sat there people watching, anticipating the adventure that lie ahead, with the usual pre-flight apprehension added in. Our flight was finally called for boarding, and although it seemed quite busy at the departure gate, once on board we saw that there were plenty of empty seats, with the plane being about two thirds full. The big bonus I found with online check in is that you can pre-select your seat up to 30 hours before departure, although when doing so we found that many seats, especially window seats, had already been taken. It turns out that people with a higher class in KLMs loyalty system get to pick their seats at the time off booking, but we still picked good seats, two right at the back but in the middle row of three seats rather than at the window. With the flight not being full there was a spare seat next to us, so we took over the two aisle seats and used the middle one for dumping stuff on (books & music etc). So, happy with our seats we were all sorted for the 9 hour flight to Vancouver.

We were soon on our way, across the North Sea and over the UK in no time, heading towards Greenland to take the more direct route to Vancouver (due to the curvature of the Earth). I have to say that I was impressed with the service offered by KLM (nothing to do with the attractiveness of the air stewardesses of course!). They seemed to know when people would want a drink, meal, snack or refreshing towel more than other airlines I've flown with over the years. The food itself was also of a good standard, and when is that ever said of airline food? There was a choice of pasta or fish, followed by soup and salad later on, all rather enjoyable. Unfortunately the plane we were on, an MD Tri-star, hadn't yet been fitted with the individual video screens which I like for the maps and other information rather than then TV programmes and films, but I was fine with my own entertainment, another of the Sharpe books and my own MP3 music/video player, an updated Creative Zen (nothing like watching highlights of Germany 1 England 5 over the Atlantic, even 6 years afterwards!). We got occasional views of the map on the big screen in between the films they were showing, and we were soon coming down over northern Canada towards the Rockies, although constant cloud obscured any sight of the ground from our limited view out of the windows.

Eventually the cloud cover broke and we got some great views of the Rocky Mountains as we began our descent to Vancouver, with some good views of the city itself as we came in to land. After 9 hours on the plane it was great to finally get off and walk about, and after a short wait to get through customs and get our bags, we were out of the airport and into a taxi to the hotel. It felt strange to be taking the taxi journey I'd taken in the other direction over two years earlier, and we even went past the hotel I'd stayed in previously, the Radisson on Granville Street. This time though Vancouver was the start of the adventure, with three weeks of trans-continental travel ahead of us. As the taxi drove down Robson Street where the hotel is, the Listel, Dan recognised the street and where the hotel would be from his looking on Google Earth before leaving. We were well impressed with the hotel, very modern and stylish, and our room was on the 'museum floor' with a selection of art on display.

After getting sorted at the hotel it was time to head out for a few beers. A late one certainly wasn't planned, as although it was 5pm local time, it was 1am back home and we'd both been up since about 3am British Summer Time, or 7pm the previous night Pacific Time. First stop was O'Douls, a modern bar which is joined on to the hotel and was where we'd be getting breakfast for the duration of our stay in Vancouver. As with the first beer in Halifax over two years previously, it was great to be sat at the bar in O'Douls, enjoying the first beer of the trans-continental adventure, contemplating what lay ahead. First up was a local beer, a pint of R&B Bohemian, very nice, followed by my favourite, Alexander Keiths India Pale Ale, fantastic stuff, so much so that I just had to have a photo taken holding the bottle and the glass either side of my smiling face!

After a few beers in there we headed down Robson Street in search of another bar, but with that part of the street being mainly shops, that was proving to be hard work until we found the Lennox pub on corner of Granville Street, a pub I'd been to on the previous trip to Vancouver. It was quite strange to be in there thinking of the previous trip, trying to fight off the jet lag with more beer. After there we went down Granville to Speak Easy, again where I'd been previously, but soon the beer, jet lag and lack of food began to kick in so we flagged down a taxi and went back to the hotel area for something to eat. There was a small Chinese cafe opposite the hotel, so had a good feed in there before going back to the hotel for some much needed sleep. Unfortunately my sleep was disturbed somewhat by Dan's snoring, something I'd become quite familiar with over the next three weeks, but the ear plugs I'd been given on a recent work trip did help alleviate it to some degree!

Friday 21st September 2007

I woke up at 6am and was up and about for 7am, and we both sent our other brother Barney a happy birthday text message, before going down to O'Douls for breakfast, opting for the Yukon breakfast (a fry up basically) which sorted us out a treat, ready for the day's sightseeing around Vancouver. The plan was to walk down to the Lookout Tower, then go to North Vancouver by ferry and catch a bus to the Capilano Suspension Bridge, the first destination being somewhere I'd been to before but was looking forward to revisiting, the second being a new experience for me as I didn't go to North Vancouver on the previous visit.

The Vancouver Lookout Tower lies on West Hastings Street near the SeaBus terminal, so was handy for the ferry we'd be getting afterwards, and was a fairly short walk from our hotel which is in a relatively central location, so it was basically along Robson Street and down Seymour Street. The observation deck is at 480 feet and is reached by an elevator on the outside of the Harbour Centre building with a glass front, which takes you up from street level in about 30 seconds. Like last time it was cloudy, but at least it wasn't raining so the 360' view was much better, and we both took plenty of pictures on our way round, spotting familiar landmarks and places we'd been and where we'd be going. I often think it's the best thing to do at the start of a visit to a city, go to the top of the highest building and have a good look around, spot the sights, get your bearings, put things into perspective and remember how peaceful it looks from above.

Once we'd finished there we went down to the SeaBus terminal, which proved to be hard to find despite having been looking down on it from Vancouver's highest building! Once there we bought a day pass for $8 (£4), which gives all day access to the city buses, SeaBus (the passenger ferry connecting downtown Vancouver and North Vancouver) and SkyTrain (a metro system that mostly runs on elevated tracks). After a short wait we were on the SeaBus ferry for the 15 minute journey across Burrard Inlet to North Vancouver, sitting at the back and watching the skyline of Downtown Vancouver get further away. Once at the other end we were straight into the bus station and caught the Number 236 bus to the Capilano Suspension Bridge, passing through some very affluent looking suburbs along the way, a very desirable place to live in my opinion. The main attraction there is naturally the bridge itself, a footbridge which is suspended 230 feet above the canyon floor and is 450 feet long, but there are numerous attractions along the way with totem poles (including one to stand in and pull a face for the camera as I did!), a First Nations carving centre, gardens, information boards, musicians in late Victorian dress (as the attraction was originally built in 1889), shops and refreshments.

The bridge is very impressive despite the large amount of other people sharing the enjoyment of it all, plenty of people doing the same as us and posing for photos in numerous places along the bridge. It does wobble a fair bit but is perfectly safe, or one assumes it is anyway! The original bridge from 1889 was constructed of hemp rope and cedar planks, this was replaced by a wire cable bridge in 1903, reinforced in 1914 with additional cables, but was completely rebuilt in 1956 with reinforced steel safely anchored in 13 tons of concrete on either side of the canyon. After taking in the various views and looking down at the Capilano River, it was time to check out the woodland walks on the other side of the canyon. Firstly the cliff top walk which follows a path through the trees, near the edge of the canyon for a while, and then the treetops walk where there are a series of bridges suspended between small platforms on the trees, some as high as 100 feet above the forest floor, so you certainly get a squirrels eye view of the rainforest.

It was all very enjoyable and made me want to keep taking photos, but then I kept remembering that photos of trees and more trees are not all that interesting, so didn't take that many in the end, just a few more of the bridge on the way back over. As we got near to the other end of the bridge I could hear a familiar tune being played and saw that three musicians dressed up in Victorian era costume were playing Swing Low Sweet Chariot, which seemed appropriate at the time given that the rugby World Cup was on, although England had got off to a nightmare start with a 36-0 defeat at the hands of South Africa before we left home. After checking out the shops it was time for a couple of beers at the cafe, but as we were sat there under the canopy it started raining heavily, making me wish I'd taken my cap with me to give some protection against the rain other than my hoodless jacket.

Still, can't let the rain get in the way of our plans, so we went across the road and waited for the bus to take us up to Grouse Mountain, where we could get a cable car to the top. It seemed to take ages for the bus to turn up, especially as the trees at the side of the road weren't really providing much shelter, but finally one did and we were on our way further up the hill to the cable car. It was still raining and looking cloudy all around, so we weren't too optimistic about the views we'd be getting, but we were there and decided to go up in case we didn't get the chance to go again, which was likely to be the case given that we only had another two days in Vancouver.

The views from the cable car were quite spectacular to start with due to the steep angle of the climb, although we couldn't see much beyond the mountainside due to the cloud. About halfway up we went into the cloud itself, reducing visibility to about 50 yards, and this was the extent of the view at the top which was immersed in the clouds. Without any kind of a view we had a bite to eat and a beer in the cafe, had a look at the clouds from the outside balcony, and then headed back down the mountain. No kind of view but at least we'd been up there, and as Dan said it was another reason to return to Vancouver one day. Once out of the cloud halfway down the mountain we got more of a glimpse of North Vancouver, and tried to envisage what the view from the top would be like on a clear day, very spectacular I imagine. Off the rails Part Three anyone?!

The bus was fairly empty to start with but soon began filling up with a variety of people, and as we passed through the picturesque suburbs and then down into North Vancouver itself, it was interesting just people watching and wondering what sort of lives the other passengers were going back to as they got off the bus at various stops. Once we'd taken the SeaBus back to Downtown we walked down Water Street to Gastown, where we found what I'd missed last time I was there, the steam powered clock, which chimes every hour. Luckily we were there at five to four so joined the other tourists in waiting for the big event of a steam powered clock chiming to mark the passing of another hour. The clock is about 20 feet high, has a clock face on each side, and has tubes on each corner. As the clock struck four it whistled the Big Ben tune through the four smaller tubes, and then blew steam like a ship through the main tube at the end, all very exciting for the couple of dozen tourists including ourselves stood there with our cameras at the ready.

Feeling content after the excitement of the steam clock, we made our way back to the hotel, stopping at a shop to buy some rum and then Malones bar on Seymour and Pender for a couple of beers, this being the bar where we went after Chinatown in 2005, so a bit more reminiscing to be done, and I think we even managed to sit at the same table as last time! After that we went back to the hotel to chill out for a bit and drink some of the Sailor Jerry's rum we'd just bought, then got sorted out and went down to our usual seats at the bar in O'Douls for a few beers. The beer brought on the hunger and we decided to try out the White Tower restaurant across the road, which was mainly Greek food, nice enough but not very good service, the jet lag was kicking in, so feeling full and tired we were back to the hotel and crashed out by 10pm (6am UK time!), with the first full day in Canada behind us.

Saturday 22nd September 2007

Having said that, I was sat up awake at 4am, willing the time to be 7am so the gym was open and I could escape Dan's snoring, when I started getting text messages from back home – my dad and some friends had gone on an ale trail by double decker bus with our favourite pub in Northallerton, the Tithe Bar, and Chris (of the previous Canada trips) kept saying how they were on the beer already, about midday that would have been back home. They found it quite amusing when I mentioned my situation. I managed to get some more sleep with the combined help of ear plugs and my MP3 player, though not at the same time, but was still down the gym at 7-30am, more through the time difference than the snoring to be honest, with my body clock (and my dad, Chris and Adrian via SMS!) telling me it was later than 7-30am!

The gym in the Listel Hotel is small but modern, containing enough there to give me a good early morning workout on the cross-trainer, treadmill and weights, whilst watching the Arsenal v Derby match live on Canadian TV, and trying to work out if I was tired, still jet-lagged, or hungover. There's also a small spa pool there but gave it a miss that day, especially when a couple of others went in to take up much of the space. After a brief but good workout I went back to the room, we had our usual Yukon breakfast in O'Douls, checked the football scores on the internet in the hotel reception (Darlo lost 1-0 at MK Dons following a last minute goal), then walked down Robson Street ready for the day's entertainment.

Our plan was to get on one of the city tour buses, something I'd never actually done before but it would be a great way of taking it easy whilst seeing more of the city with some additional tourist information along the way. After numerous text messages from home about the Tithe Bar Northallerton Ale Trail around the area, we thought it was time to kick off the Vancouver Ale Trail, so stopped off at a bar called the Cactus Bar on Robson Street (which we'd missed on the first night) for a couple of beers to wash down that breakfast. With the weather being quite clear and sunny we wandered around for a bit, went into Sears and The Bay where I'd bought some clothes on my previous visit, and returned to the part of Robson Street where the "Big Bus" picks up from, deciding to have a beer in the 72 Sports Bar first.

This was a smart looking bar situated upstairs and set back slightly from the street, and was full of TVs showing mainly baseball and American football. I was hoping that they would have coverage of the Toronto FC match that was being played that afternoon, but they couldn't get the channel it was being shown on so had to make do with the stop-start rugby with helmets and padding, and rounders with a big bat. As you can tell I'm not keen on either sport, although the latter is perhaps more bearable. The only popular North American sport I like is hockey, but they were still in the pre-season at that point, with the regular season being another week away. It seemed like a good bar anyway.

After a beer in there it was time to get our tickets for Big Bus from a small shop across the road, and after waiting for what seemed like an eternity one of the open topped buses pulled up and we were on our way. A few covered buses had gone past but with the weather being nice we wanted one of the open top buses, these being covered for the front quarter and open the rest. We were greeted with a pre-recorded "welcome to Big Bus", with the tour information being delivered by a recording as we travelled along, all very informative and timed with where we were along the route. We headed east first of all, went round the library before heading through Chinatown (where we had the Chinese meal in 2005) and into Gastown. The bus stopped here for a break so all passengers had to get off and wait for one of the two buses parked up to start off again. With that it was time for another beer, so we went to the Steamworks Brewing Company just up the road, sitting outside and enjoying the dry and sunny weather. It would have been a good day to have gone up Grouse Mountain which was almost free of cloud, certainly much less than the previous day, but we'd made our choice for the day so went back to the bus and got places on the back seat.

As we were sat there waiting for other passengers to board, we watched the crowds around the steam clock we'd seen on the previous day, and listened to a great busker who was playing some kind of ukulele, blowing on some sort of high pitched mouth organ, and singing some Chinese type song whilst encouraging the crowds to dance along! Difficult to describe really, but it was very entertaining and I'm glad I took a short video clip to remember it by.

After that bit of live entertainment we were on our way again, going along the Waterfront by Canada Place, then heading across downtown, over the Burrard Bridge to the Granville Island area, then back across the Granville Bridge, again passing the hotel where I'd stayed on my previous visit. After doing a small loop we were heading along the English Bay area, passing Sunset Beach, English Bay Beach and Second Beach. This seemed like a very popular area, with quite a few people chilling out along the tree-lined shores of English Bay, all very picturesque. The bus then went through Stanley Park, which was very well looked after and a great retreat from the downtown area, with a series of paths making it great for walking around. We stayed on the bus and soon found ourselves going back up Robson Street, so got off at the stop just before the Listel Hotel.

It had been a great way to spend a couple of hours, chilling out on the bus, taking in the sights of what is a very scenic and vibrant city, whilst getting the pre-recorded tour information along the way, and it was also a good way to get more of a feel for the city and to appreciate where different areas are in relation to the map. By now it was late afternoon and time to resume the Vancouver ale trail, so after a quick wash and change it was time to hit the town. We started with a couple in the local, taking our usual seats at the bar in O'Douls, then decided to head across the road to Fogg and Suds, which was located upstairs opposite the hotel, with a fine view of the street. We had dinner there and a few beers, nice bar and nice waitress, but decided to try and walk off the fullness from the meal, a whole 200 yards to Shenanigans. This pub was quite large but the decor and some of the clientele made it seem like a cross between a working men's club and a British seaside cafe! After there we walked a bit further, down Granville Street to a smart little bar called Granville Room. Much classier in there, and feeling bloated from the food and beer Dan went onto vodka and Red Bull, and I went onto rum and coke. Sorted us out, especially with the large measures, both felt much more lively.

After there we went into Doolins pub, which was a bit more of a British style pub, and then went into the Republic night club. We were about the first people in there and it was almost empty to start with, but it soon filled up. The thing is though, the rum and coke started playing havoc with my stomach, too much coke I reckon, nothing to do with the rum or beer that preceded it, which is why if I drive on a night out I often drink alcohol free lager or soda water rather than a soft drink, too sweet for my liking. Anyway, needless to say, I paid a visit to the 'restroom' where the contents of my stomach were reintroduced to the outside world through the same way they went in. Quite frustrating as I wasn't particularly drunk and wanted to stay out, but after that experience there wasn't one thing I could have drunk apart from water, so we got a taxi back to the hotel. I crashed out but with it still being quite early, about 11pm, Dan went down the road for a drink whilst I got some sleep, ready for the first train journey the next day.

Sunday 23rd September 2007

I was awake early so went down to the gym again, this time making use of the spa pool after a short workout, which was very relaxing. After the usual breakfast and our final visit to O'Douls we checked out at 11-30, and with six hours to kill before the train left we sat outside a nearby cafe where we had a few cups of coffee and watched the world go by, reflecting on our days in Vancouver. The place had certainly left an impression on the both of us, and it has to be one of the most beautiful cities in the world. You don't need to go far to get a view of mountains or water, the streets are wide, although there are plenty of high rise buildings they don't seem as imposing as in other big cities such as New York and Toronto, the place has a more chilled out feel to it than other large cities, all of which left us both wanting to visit again someday. Oh, and there's the desire to go up Grouse Mountain when it's not hidden in the clouds!

With time to kill there's only so long that an Englishman can go without a beer, so we walked down Robson Street to the 72 Sports Bar for a couple of beers and a light lunch, again surrounded by TVs with the sport that should be called handball rather than football. After that we got a taxi down to the train station, still with hours to spare, but we had to get our passes and reservation tickets sorted. Once we'd done that, and I'd reminisced about my arrival there on the previous trip, we went for a wander and had a quick look at the science centre around the corner, buying some illustrated maps in the shop, before heading back to the station area and having a beer in the Ivanhoe pub next to the station. This wasn't like any of the bars downtown, and seemed to be more like all pubs next to train stations around the world, with a more rough and ready feel to it, and a cross section of locals drinking the afternoon away.

It was finally approaching boarding time, and after waiting around in the station with the temperature rising, we boarded the train at 4-45pm ready for the 5-30pm departure. There were two carriages allocated to Comfort Class passengers, which are those who have reclining seats rather than sleeping accommodation. You can upgrade to sleeper class for parts of the journey, but it effectively doubles the price so we decided against it, and I'd found it okay last time. We were soon all settled and on our way through the suburbs of Vancouver, which is far bigger than the downtown area we'd spent the last few days in. It was a clear evening and we were soon out of suburbia and into the forested countryside, and that view out of the train window as we left Vancouver is one that I shall always remember. There were a few rivers along the way, before the light faded and our attention turned to books, music and beer from the cafe car. With us having two reclining seats each, which have a very generous leg room and a fold up leg rest, and the staff giving us blankets and pillows, it was easy to get comfortable enough to sleep although I usually had to change position every half hour to stop some part of the seat sticking in my neck or back.

Monday 24th September 2007

I woke up a few times but managed a reasonable night's sleep, then with daylight approaching and us being in the Rocky Mountains I decided to have a quick wash, get a coffee and sit in the dome car. It was quite cloudy at first, but there were a few others in the dome car enjoying the scenery, including an Australian woman who liked the sound of her own voice too much for that time of morning! I saw a black bear with its cub at one point, tried taking a photo but came out blurred, but at least I'd finally seen a bear in the wild after missing out last time. As the light got stronger and the cloud cleared away, I began taking more photos including one of a waterfall which I later realised I'd snapped on my phone camera on the previous trip, that time in the evening and travelling in the opposite direction. I returned to the seats where Dan was now awake, and by now the scenery was becoming quite spectacular, which presented plenty of photo opportunities.

With the last trip across Canada being in the spring, the landscape was quite barren in appearance at times, with the trees either being still covered in snow, as was the case in Nova Scotia, the grass was looking very faded, or the trees were a dull green and sometimes brown colour. This time however, in early autumn, or fall as it's called in North America, the landscape was much more colourful, with spectacular contrasts of varying degrees of green and yellow. Mount Robson was soon in view, the highest mountain in the Canadian Rockies at 12,972ft, we passed Moose Lake which looked very green in appearance, and we were now truly in the majestic and awe inspiring land that I'd enjoyed so much last time and was looking forward to experiencing again. With the train passing into Alberta we put our watches forward as we went onto Mountain Standard Time, and we were approaching Jasper ready for the next part of the adventure.

Chapter 2 – Alberta

It seemed to take ages to arrive in Jasper, but with the amazing scenery all around and us being in no rush to get anywhere, that didn't really matter. I was really looking forward to arriving in Jasper, remembering my reaction last time when I'd got off the train, when I ooked around and said "wow". Such is the impression the place left on me last time it almost felt like a homecoming, which I guess makes Jasper one of those places in the world that are really special to me, where the surroundings give a real boost to my feelings of well being, where I feel relaxed yet excited, at home yet in a far off land. So in light of that, it felt great to step off that train, walk along the platform area (which isn't a raised platform as such, it's all at track level) and take in the familiar sights of Jasper, surrounded by the rocky, snow capped, tree covered mountains in all directions.

It was shortly before midday when we arrived, the weather had become quite sunny, and we headed straight to our hotel, the good old Whistlers Inn where we'd stayed last time I was there. With us being a little early the room wasn't ready, so we went into the bar for a couple of beers, where I took a photo on my phone and sent it to Chris saying "remember this place?". The room was soon ready and we were pleasantly surprised to find that we'd been allocated one of the suites on the first floor, which overlooked the front of the hotel, giving a fantastic view of the centre of Jasper and the surrounding mountains. The room itself was great and had a lounge area with sofa and table, as well as the usual two double beds and bathroom, all of which added to the feeling of homeliness about the place. A great place to chill out for a few days before travelling to the big cities in the east.

After spending the night on the train and changing time zones (that one hour difference can really take it out of you!) we were feeling a bit 'train-lagged', so got showered and changed before heading out to enjoy the delights of Jasper. It was great to be wandering the streets of Jasper again, renewing my memories of the place, and first of all we walked down Patricia Street which runs adjacent to Connaught Drive, the main street on which the train station is located, before turning back onto Connaught Drive when we got to L&Ws restaurant, where I'd eaten during the last visit.

By now we were in need of some lunch, so went to the small Pizza Hut franchise around the corner from L&Ws, where we had some very tasty pizza. Next stop was Sundog Tours to check out the adventures that were available. A trip up Whistlers Mountain on the cable car was a must, especially as it was still closed during my last visit, and we decided we'd hire a car on one of the days and drive down the Icefields Parkway to the Athabasca Glacier, which we'd driven past last time on the trip to Banff. We also fancied some kind of rafting trip, or maybe just hiring a boat on one of the nearby lakes. Loaded up with leaflets we wandered back along

Patricia Street to the internet café, where I took the opportunity to uploads some photos onto the travel blog I'd set up (www.statravelblogs.com/mash), this being done using the same site as Mel & Sue on their 2005 trip that I mentioned earlier. Although ours was a three week trip and not a whole year, it's a great way of keeping a few people informed of our travels, and allows photos and videos to be uploaded, has location maps to update, as well as blog entries and a message board.

Once we'd finished up there we walked back round to Connaught Drive and went into the Jasper Brewing Company for some beers. As the name suggests, this place has a selection of home brewed beers, along with others from the area, and included a quite distinctive honey beer which Dan tried. He was quite impressed with the beers but I was more keen on the standard Keith's and Kokanee lagers, rather than one's which have a funny taste to them! We had a nice little spot sat by the window, watching people walk past and marvelling at the mountains, so it was a nice chilled out couple of hours spent there. After that we went for a walkabout around the centre of the town, looking at various shops, then back to the hotel room for a bit before going downstairs to the Whistlers Inn bar for a few more beers. By now we were getting peckish after the fullness from the pizzas had worn off and the beer had taken effect, so we went into the small supermarket on Patricia Street for some munchies before going back to the room where I ended up crashing out early, but Dan went across the road for to the Athabasca Hotel for a few beers and ended up staying out until 2am.

Tuesday 25th September 2007

With my early night I was awake early in the morning, so got up at about 7am when it was still dark and went for a walk around the block, stopping for a coffee and a look at the internet in the Soft Rock internet café on Connaught Drive, quite near to Pizza Hut and the Jasper Brewing Company. I watched the sun rise over the mountains, a calming yet inspirational sight, walked back to the hotel where Dan was still asleep after his late night, so I walked round the block again, this time stopping at another internet café called No Just Mail in one of the small streets connect Connaught Drive and Patricia Street. After that I went back to the room where Dan was still catching up on sleep, so I went down the hotel restaurant for breakfast. The service there was appalling, with two snotty middle aged women serving, they took ages to take my order, they refused to let someone take a table for breakfast as it was two minutes past ten and argued in front of the handful of customers, and they were not very attentive. Still, the food was okay, an omelette with hash browns which filled me up, and after that I went along to the bike shop on Patricia Street, in a much better state of mind that on my last visit there in 2005!

It was hiring a bike there in 2005 which inspired me to buy a bike back home later that year, a decision I'm so glad I made with my mountain bike now being my mode of transport for work (okay, only half a mile, but it's quicker than walking and saves on petrol!), and also it's got me out and about around the local country lanes and hills, as well as doing the C2C route from Whitehaven to Tynemouth in 2008, the Hadrian's Cycleway from Ravenglass to Newcastle in 2009, and the Coast and Castles route from Newcastle to Edinburgh in 2010. With that in mind I planned to hire a bike for the week, and keep it locked up outside the hotel. The bikes were all pretty much the same and although it seemed good in 2005, it now seemed poor in comparison to my Giant Rock bike back home, which is nothing flash but I've become accustomed to it.

I biked up to the top end of the town, then started going up Pyramid Lake Road, easy enough climb but with me being the only person up there apart from the odd passing car, bear paranoia hit me and I headed back into town! I was convinced that I could hear a bear but I think it was just my imagination! The bike was making an annoying squeaking noise whenever I was freewheeling, so I took it back and changed it for another one. The second bike wasn't much better though as the brakes were squeaky, but I decided to put up with it and biked back up Pyramid Lake Road, going a bit further this time before bear paranoia struck again, then around to the southern end of town. It seemed to be mainly seasonal accommodation here, as in the summer season the town's population can increase significantly from the permanent population of around 5,000. I also got good views of Whistlers Mountain from here and the Jasper Tramway, which told me that it was time to go back to the hotel as surely Dan was up and ready for going out.

Despite the annoying noises made by the bike, and the paranoia about bears when going out of town, it had been enjoyable cycling around town, seeing a bit more of the residential areas, enjoying the fresh air and mountainous scenery. As I got back to the hotel the heavens opened and it began to pour down with rain, which put off any ideas of spending the day cycling. Back in the room and Dan was up and about, and as the rain quickly stopped we decided to take the trip to Whistlers Mountain, taking our chances with the cloud overhead. After the experience in Vancouver, the last thing we wanted was to take another cable car ride into the clouds, but after the rainfall it was looking quite clear around the mountain.

We'd booked our tickets via Sun Dog Adventure Tours, who picked us up from the totem pole next to the train station, then took us and a handful of others on the short journey to the Jasper Tramway. The tramway was opened in 1964, and the Lower Station, at 4279ft above sea level, contains a well stocked gift shop as well as the ticket office, where our Sun Dog representative collected our tickets that we'd already paid for. After a short wait we got into the cable car and were on our way, along with about a dozen others and an employee of the Jasper Tramway, providing details about trip to the top and the changing scenery below us on the mountain. We were stood at the back of the cable car, same as on the Grouse Mountain cable car, but this time the cloud had cleared and the views were fantastic. It was fascinating watching the vegetation below change from dense tree cover to rocky mountain and then snow, and after about 8 minutes we reached the Upper Station at 7472ft above sea level. The Upper Station has a shop on the lower level and cafe on the upper level, with a viewing platform on either side of the shop and embarkation area. We went out on the right hand side as you face away from the mountain, where the temperature was posted as 2'C on a small board with a clock and last operating times of the cable car.

The view in all directions was simply marvellous. Straight ahead was the Jasper town site, which is in a kind of inverted L-shape when looking from Whistlers Mountain, with the railway and main roads going through the town before meandering away through the deep valleys. Beyond and above Jasper, and further away than I thought when I began cycling that way earlier on, was Pyramid Lake, and Pyramid Mountain beyond that. Over to the left was a deep tree covered valley where we'd come along on the train from Vancouver. To the right we could see the Icefields Parkway, the road down towards Banff.

Behind us was the summit of Whistlers Mountain, which looked to be about a mile away up quite a steep climb, perfectly manageable but only if properly dressed for it. I'd decided to wear my newly purchased 'Mountain' walking trousers, which were fine but a bit thin, and my shirt, jacket and baseball cap didn't give much protection from the wind either. Dan had jeans and a cagoule on, so again not enough protection to go to the top. Although the temperature was posted as 2'C at the station, it certainly felt colder when we walked out the back where we were exposed to the wind. After talking to a couple from Durham who were travelling across Canada in a camper van (sounds like another trip for the future!), we went for a wander behind the tramway station, taking photos and videos, and enjoying the snow. Next time I'll take my Berghaus coat, jumper, woolly hat, gloves and leggings, then I'll go to the summit, as a few people who were better dressed for it did. So as with the mountain at Vancouver, another reason to go back to Canada!

Despite the cold I loved it up there. It was so refreshing, taking in all that amazing scenery and fresh air. We'd been watching the Weather Channel in the hotel and saw that there was a bit of a heat wave in the east, with it being 25'C in Toronto and even hotter in New York. As I stood there in freezing temperatures, with a slight fall of snow, taking in the surroundings, it felt strange to think that in a week's time we'd be in the hustle and bustle of downtown Toronto with temperatures in the mid-twenties. Even more reason to take more photos to remember it by, so this time we went to the platform on the other side of the station, where the temperature was posted as 0'C rather than 2'C shown on the other side! It was one of those moments, in one of those places, when once photos and videos were taken, words were said, which were all helping to appreciate the surroundings and preserve the memory, all that had to put aside and the focus was switched to what I could see, what I could feel, what I could smell, and what I could hear. It was a real moment to just enjoy the surroundings and forget about anything else.

After that it was time for a coffee upstairs, and it was one of the most scenic places for a coffee I've been, sat in the cafe which is right on the edge of the mountain, looking down the mountainside where the cable cars go, and beyond to Jasper and the surrounding mountains and valleys. In terms of the altitude and the quality of the view, it was comparable to the cafe above Lyseboten in Norway that I'd been to in 2005, or even the cafe in the CN Tower in Toronto, but with a completely different kind of view to the latter. Of the three though, Whistlers Mountain is definitely my favourite.

Once we'd taken enough pictures, breathed in enough fresh air, and seen enough spectacular scenery, it was time to head back down the mountain, satisfied at having done some awe inspiring sightseeing in one of the most beautiful places I've ever been to. After the short ride down in the cable car we spent some time in the gift shop as we waited for the ride back to Jasper, then went to L&Ws restaurant for a good slap up meal. I'd been there twice before on my previous visit and thoroughly enjoyed both meals, and I'm pleased to say that this time was no different, with us both having filling and enjoyable meals. The plan for the next day was to hire a car and drive down the Icefields Parkway to the Athabasca glacier, so we didn't want to be out drinking much that night. Instead, we walked back to the hotel, and took advantage of the comfortable accommodation and chilled out in the room for the evening, ready for the next day's adventure.

Wednesday 26th September 2007

Wednesday morning and the weather was looking brighter, so after breakfast in Smittys next to the hotel, another omelette with hash browns, we went over to the train station to hire a car. There are three hire car companies operating from Jasper train station, and all were quite busy. We chose National car hire and were hoping for a nice 4x4 gas guzzler to cruise through the mountains in, but the last one had just been hired out so we ended up with a nice little gold Toyota Solara automatic convertible, later described by my friend Mel as a 'pimp mobile' after I'd put a picture of it on our travel blog! It was a decent little car though and we were soon on our way out of Jasper, listening to Dan's New Order CD that he'd bought in Vancouver, and heading down Highway 93, stopping after a few miles at the toll gate to pay the park toll.

The distance to the Athabasca glacier was about 65 miles but we were in no hurry with a 90kmph / 55mph speed limit, and above all the amazing scenery to enjoy. This is what I'd been looking forward to, and after telling my brother so much about the scenery along the Icefields Parkway it was good to see him appreciating the all round views. That road is such a joy to drive, it makes driving a real pleasure, an event in itself rather than just a means to get somewhere (www.icefieldsparkway.ca). Around every corner is a picture post card view, snow capped mountains towering above, endless forests with varying colours, the Athabasca river meandering through the valleys. The road has a continuous lay by as well as some larger parking areas, so stopping to take photos of the majestic scenery is no problem. The only problem was that the weather was getting a bit overcast and we had a little bit of rain on the way down, but that had stopped by the time we arrived at the Columbia Icefields visitors centre and the skies were looking brighter again.

The Columbia Icefields is located on the boundary of the Jasper and Banff National Parks, and the visitors centre itself is located in the Jasper Park, facing the Athabasca Glacier. The centre was packed with other tourists, especially Japanese, and after buying our tickets for the glacier tour we went outside to wait for the bus. The conventional bus took us away from the centre towards the glacier, and then we transferred to a specially designed Brewster Ice Explorer bus, with six huge wheels which are about five feet across, and it was this one which took us onto the glacier itself. Before getting onto the glacier we descended the steepest passenger carrying hill in North America, being 32% or 18 degrees, which as the driver explained was safe due to the transmission lock in operation.

It was a really fascinating tour which took us onto the glacier to a specially cleared area of the ice where we could get off the bus and walk around. The importance of staying within the cleared area was stressed several times, as cracks and crevasses in the ice are common and are often covered up by snow. It was intriguing to hear that melt water from the Columbia Icefields feeds streams and rivers which flow into the Arctic, Pacific and Atlantic oceans, the latter via the Hudson Bay. Indeed Mount Snowdome, on the edge of the Icefields, could lay claim to this feat itself, with melt water draining to all three oceans. The Icefields covers 200 square miles with solid ice up to 1200 feet deep, and is the largest sub-polar body of ice in North America.

There were several other 'buses' there, so quite a few people scattered about the safe area, although inevitably a few walked a few feet beyond this cleared area which had been fully checked for any holes in the ice. It was a great opportunity for taking photos, the most memorable being those I took looking up the mountains to the side with separate glaciers clearly visible, one of which has pride of place on my wall at home. It was fairly cold but not unbearable (refreshing as I like to say), and I was glad I took my sunglasses to combat the glare off the snow, with the weather being quite sunny by then. They also came in handy when gusts of wind kept blowing snow along the surface of the glacier creating temporary blizzard like conditions, when added to the light snow that fell occasionally. As with Whistlers Mountain the day before, I took in the surroundings with the thought of the hot weather that we'd likely be experiencing a week later in the east, enjoying the cool, fresh, clean air and awe inspiring landscape.

All in all a great experience and after around half an hour there we were back on the six monster-truck-wheeled bus. At the transfer area we had a short wait for the conventional bus, which gave us opportunity to take more photos, including one of an old style bus which used to be used for the glacier tours, this being basically a converted road bus with tracks on the undercarriage instead of wheels, apparently not very comfortable according to the driver of the modern day replacement. We were soon back at the visitors centre, which is open from the start of April until the end of October – it was interesting to hear that when the staff arrive to reopen after the winter the snow can be over 20 feet high, so I guess it's no wonder it's closed, there's no way they could get to the glacier through all that.

With Dan having driven down there it was my turn to drive, something I was looking forward to. I'd never driven a left hand drive car, never driven an automatic, and my only drive on the right hand side of the road was 5 miles in Norway in a British hire car. Furthermore, I'd never had the pleasure of doing the driving myself in such fantastic scenery. It was strange at first with there being no gear stick, but I soon got used it and being on the other side of the road wasn't a problem, although I did tend to drift to the middle of the road a bit. The drive was great, especially as by now the sky was clear and the afternoon sun gave the perfect light to bring out the contrasting colours of the landscape around us, so after taking photos of the road ahead giving us something extra to remember the drive by, we stopped and went down the embankment to take some photos next to the Athabasca River. In between scanning the area for bears, we took some great photos there which captured the beauty of the surroundings, enhanced by the closeness to the river with its inviting but freezing clear blue water.

After our photo shoot we were off again, but we'd decided to take a detour by taking Route 93A, a quieter road which would take us up towards the Marmont Basin ski resort. It was fantastic driving along there, with the sun shining and bringing out the colour of the trees around us, the roof down, very little traffic so we could continue to stop and take photos as we pleased. The 93A was a narrower road without markings, and felt more isolated and part of the forest around us, which made us a little more wary when stopping in case a bear suddenly appeared. We really wanted to see a bear but not too close up! We turned off up the mountain towards the Marmont Basin ski resort, with the road winding its way steadily up the hill, giving us more and more of a view as we progressed up the mountainside. Eventually we came to a barrier across the road as the ski resort was closed, so without a key to the barrier that obviously only those working there had, we turned around back down the mountain after swapping driving again.

By now we were just a few miles outside of Jasper, and were originally thinking of getting a boat out at Pyramid Lake, but with the time getting on we decided to have a drive up there to check the place out and then go back early in the morning before taking the car back. The journey to Pyramid Lake from Jasper was further than I remembered, so was glad I didn't keep cycling up there the day before. We're only talking about four miles, but the road is quiet and I was paranoid about bears! It was great when we arrived at the lake though, as last time I was there in early April 2005 it was still frozen over and the hotel next to the lake was still closed for the winter. This time the lake was a beautiful deep blue colour, surrounded by trees of various autumnal shades of green, yellow and orange, and a clear blue sky above. It was perfect for taking more photographs, so we walked out on to the small jetty to take some pictures, then had a look at the boat hiring place at the hotel. I was happy with a rowing boat, having enjoyed rowing around a fjord in Norway in 2004 and 2005, but Dan was up for getting a canoe, something I had never tried before and was wary of how unstable they are.

After some time up there we went back into Jasper, parked the car, got changed and went out for some dinner, choosing the Chinese restaurant on Connaught Drive after a couple of beers in the downstairs Downstream bar first, where I'd been on the previous visit. We took our time in restaurant, had a few beers and a nice meal, but felt far too full to keep on drinking so went back to the hotel around 9pm. It had a been a great day, one that stands out now as one of the highlights of the trip, a day of constant spectacular scenery that normally one only sees on TV, the internet, or in books. We'd both taken plenty of photos that day to capture the delight of our surroundings, and I was so inspired by the results that I've since created a mini-Jasper gallery on my living room wall of some of the photos taken that week, including Pyramid Lake, Icefields Parkway, Athabasca Glacier, Athabasca River, Whistlers Inn and Whistlers Mountain.

Thursday 27th September 2007

We were up fairly early the next day, and after some breakfast we drove up to Pyramid Lake to hire out a boat. I'd given in to Dan's desire to hire a canoe rather than a good old sturdy rowing boat, persuaded slightly after seeing the larger size two man canoes available. Once we'd paid up and got the paddles we went to the lakeside, dragged a canoe the water's edge, and began to get in. I got in first, the canoe wobbled a bit but seemed okay, then as Dan was getting behind me the whole thing wobbled a lot more and then suddenly tipped over to the side, sending me into about two feet of water. I was unable to get my leg out in time so stuck my hand out to stop me falling right over, which hurt my thumb a bit, but worse than that was the fact that I was soaked. I didn't have any special outdoor clothing other than my walking trousers, the only jacket I had was my £200 Aquascutum jacket, and I had my camera, phone and wallet in my pockets. The fact that we tipped over wasn't so bad, it's just what I was wearing and what I had in my pockets that bothered me. But once we'd gotten ashore and dragged the canoe back onto the side of the like, we saw the funny side and laughed about it. "Told you we should've got a rowing boat" I said.

It certainly made good entertainment for those in the hotel having breakfast, looking out of the window and seeing a couple of big Englishmen tip their canoe and fall into the lake. But as we said at the time, better to tip over there than in the middle of the lake! As it was I was in the water for little more than a second, so my wallet was just damp and would soon dry out, the camera was just damp and still worked fine, and the phone was a little more wet but would soon dry out. Needless to say we gave up on the canoe after that and got a rowing boat instead, much safer. We spent about half an hour rowing down the lake, it was good given the scenery but I was still quite wet and couldn't seem to keep the boat straight, even though I managed fine in Norway on my previous rowing boat outings. Still, glad we'd made the effort to get up and give it a go, even if we did get soaked (well, I did, Dan just got the bottom of his legs wet being in the shallower water). After the outing on the lake we went back to the hotel to get showered and changed, after taking the car back to the car hire place.

With no car, no bike, and the weather not looking too good, we didn't really have any plans for the day so initially just wandered down the road looking in the various shops and going to the internet café. It was at this point that it began to rain heavily, the temperature was noticeably colder, and there was me in just a shirt and cap to keep me warm and dry. Now I was really wishing that I'd brought my windproof and waterproof Berghaus coat that I'd taken out of my rucksack at the last minute before leaving home! So, there was only one thing for it – the pub! We walked down Connaught Drive past the tourist information centre to the De'd Dog pub, which is part of the Astoria Hotel. It was fairly quiet in there but it was only around 1pm, and after getting our beers from a delightful barmaid we sat on the comfy armchairs at the back of the pub to start a day of leisurely drinking. After a tasty and filling lunch we had a go on the 'Big Buck Hunter' arcade game, where you pick up the plastic gun and proceed with shoot various wildlife that appear on the screen. Great fun! By late afternoon it was Jagermeister time, followed by more beer, and eventually after some five hours in there it was time to move on. We went in to the O'Sheas bar, part of the Athabasca Hotel where Dan had been on the Monday night and I'd been two year previous, and on the way in were greeted by another nice barmaid who thought we were twins. "Do I look that old?" was my reply (I'm six years younger!).

As with the first visit to the Whistlers and Downstream bars, it was funny being in O'Sheas again after the time spent there on the previous trip. The pub had 'Big Buck Hunter' so we had another go on that, before settling down to some more beers. It was good just chilling out, drinking fine Canadian lager, and talking about everything from the trip so far to the trip ahead of us, previous travels to future travels, work, home, family, friends, women, football, beer, food, politics. Everything basically! By 9pm we were fairly drunk after 8 hours on the beer, and quite hungry with it being 7 hours since our lunch, so the plan of action was that I go and get some food whilst Dan goes for the drink. I walked down to the Kentucky Fried Chicken franchise that was part of the Pizza Hut shop, bought loads of fried chicken, by which time it was pouring down outside and rather than get soaked I asked the staff to order me a taxi back to the hotel. We're only talking about 300 yards but I was drunk and not wanting to get wet with my bucket of chicken and being without my jacket, so was happy to pay the five dollars to the taxi driver (I think I just gave him that much feeling embarrassed at how short the journey was!). So, back to the hotel not as wet as I would have been, Dan had got some vodka, so we stuffed our faces, drank vodka, listened to tunes and eventually crashed out, having had a fine day of drinking, eating, and falling in lakes!

Friday 28th September 2007

I woke up feeling very thirsty having run out of water, so got up at 8-30am and went to the shop to buy things to hopefully cure a rather bad hangover. I got some water, milk and orange, went back to the hotel, drank some orange and was sick in bathroom, feeling even worse than before. This was clearly not going to be a very active day. But then that was the great thing about our room, the hotel and surroundings. With the two double beds, sofa, armchairs, TV, music, books, magazine, view of the small town centre and mountains above, it was the perfect place to chill out and let a hangover pass. We eventually ventured out and went to the Jasper Brewing Company for some lunch, but I was that rough I didn't have any beer, drinking coffee instead. Some soup and pasta made me feel a bit better but was still feeling a bit dodgy, so I stayed off the beer.

After lunch we went to the internet cafe and then to some shops, where I bought an 8 inch high totem pole which now has pride of place in my living room, and then back to the hotel. The rest of the day was spent in the room, I felt a bit guilty being too ill to drink on our last night in Jasper but I really couldn't stomach another beer, but eventually we went to the shop to buy some food before returning to the hotel. So, our last night in Jasper, and my first beer free day, although I still managed some vodka just to keep the alcohol system topped up!

Saturday 29th September 2007

Saturday 29th September and the day marking the start of a 53 hour train journey had arrived. No two day break in Winnipeg this time, it would be over two days solid on the train. I was up at 8-30am again although this time with no hangover and thankfully feeling much better, and whilst waiting for Dan to get up I went to the internet cafe to watch the latest football scores. It was about 9-15am by the time I was there which was 4-15pm back in England, seemed to be going well with Darlo winning 1-0 against Peterborough, but they conceded a last minute equaliser. Bugger! After that it was back to the hotel and then we went to Smittys for our last Jasper breakfast, this time we'd both had enough of hash browns and had breakfast without them.

We checked out of the hotel, leaving our luxurious chill out room with the fantastic views, went to the station but heard that the train was running 40 minutes late. Only one thing for it, a final pint in Jasper in the Whistlers Inn. No other customers in there, but an enjoyable pint nonetheless, with 'Ring of fire' and 'beyond the sea' playing over the sound system. Back to the station, and a country and western band were entertaining the people sat around waiting for the train, including a variation of the Johnny Cash song 'Jackson' with 'Jasper' being sung instead, so now every time I hear that song I think of the Jasper version I heard that day. The train finally arrived, we got a couple of double seats opposite each other at the end of a carriage, and left Jasper at about 1pm. The first hour was spent admiring the scenery and taking photos, something that one can never tire of in Jasper National Park. The couple sat in front of me spotted a bear, then the conductor spotted another, but I didn't see either. I was still in awe at the mountains all around us, even after a week of it, their majestic beauty never ceases to amaze. The only problem was that there was a very irritating noise coming from below where we were sat, whenever the train turned there was a loud grating, squeaking noise, which became quite annoying. If we changed seats we'd end up being sat apart, and would still probably hear it even if not as much, plus the fact the location of our seats was good, being at the end of the carriage, so we decided to stay put.

I put some music on, opting for Johnny Cash, seeing as it reminded me of the drive to Banff on the last trip, and we'd just heard a country and western band singing a version of Jackson at the train station. The music seemed perfect for the scenery, and when Highwayman came on, which Cash sung along with Kris Kristofferson, Waylon Jennings and Willie Nelson, the song jumped out as being the song of the trip, just as Baba O Reilly by The Who did on the previous trip. Whenever I listen to it now, I always think of the train through the Rockies, as well as the rest of the trip, especially as I made a video slide show of the trip on my laptop with that as the soundtrack. It was enjoyable sat listening to the music, admiring the scenery, and drinking some nice cold cans of Kokanee from the buffet car.

As we passed through Hinton, the gateway to the Rockies, the mountains were soon behind us, replaced by rolling tree covered hills that seemed to go on forever, with many of the trees displaying a fine autumnal display of colour. It was sad to be leaving the mountains and the relaxation of Jasper, with Vancouver already a week behind us, but we had nearly two weeks of Toronto, New York and Boston to look forward to yet. The scenery soon became more uniform without the mountains towering above, but with over 50 hours of travel ahead of us we could only sit back and admire the view. One thing that seemed funny as we were passing through some random scenery, with little of note, was a man sat on the grass embankment, in what seemed like the middle of nowhere, just watching the world go by. Well, watching the train go by. I thought we must be near a station or village, but nothing at all, until we passed a CN sign which said "Big Eddy", which just seemed to be planted there randomly, as there were still no roads or buildings around. Bizarre!

The landscape became much flatter once we were away from the Rockies and getting towards Edmonton, but still fascinating nonetheless. We eventually got to Edmonton just after 5pm, where, after reversing into the station on a different line, we had a half hour stop and time for some fresh air. I was hoping to get some decent food there, but had forgotten just how basic the shop is there, selling mainly sweets and tacky souvenirs. The station itself is three miles north of downtown Edmonton, so there's nothing within walking distance, and after taking a few photos we got back onto the train ready to settle in for the night. I'd like to visit Edmonton some day, I've stopped there twice for half an hour at the train station and just seen the tall skyscrapers from a distance, so it would be good to walk among them one day. Edmonton also has the world's biggest shopping centre, the West Edmonton Mall, so that would be a day's entertainment. Maybe next time I do a coast to coat rail trip I'll have a couple of days there before moving on to the Rockies. Another reason to go back to Canada!

We were soon on our way out of Edmonton and it quickly got dark, although it was a very clear, moonlit night. Without the scenery to look at tiredness soon set in, so eventually we drifted off to sleep, waking up when other trains were passing, or when we stopped at red lights, or when we had a stop at Saskatoon. It was quiet on there though, apart from the odd bit or snoring from various people and the squeaking noise below, and I managed a reasonable night's sleep, waking up at around 6-30am.

Sunday 30th September 2007

As it was getting light I went to the washroom to have a quick wash and brush my teeth, good to feel reasonably clean on such a long trip, and then went for a coffee to wake me up. We were now into the province of Manitoba, on Central Time, so I put my watch ahead an hour making us six hours behind the UK. The scenery was very flat, open prairies stretching as far as the eye could see. We went through Portage la Prairie, which the train staff informed us that it's the geographic centre of North America. We passed through a few more small towns, which looked quite nice once you get beyond the immediate vicinity of the railway, also very quiet but then it was Sunday morning in rural Manitoba. As I looked at the passing towns and villages on our route through the prairies, I thought that it would be good to see such towns in more detail one day, which suggests that a trans-Canadian road trip is on the cards for the future!

The train arrived in Winnipeg at 11-45 where we would stop for an hour, so everyone got off and we initially had a look out the back of the station, where some people wandered off to what looked like a shopping centre. Me and Dan went back into the station and went to the small snack bar near the main entrance to the station, where I'd been sat with Chris two years previous as we waited for the train to Jasper. It was quite nice sat there having a cup of tea and a sandwich, admiring the architecture of the entrance hall to the station with its dome shaped roof. Oh, and the female students sat about ten yards away! After our breakfast we walked out the front of the station, where I'd been surprised at the heat when arriving there on the previous visit, and crossed the busy multi-lane road, via the crossing which only gives enough time to get halfway across each carriageway before send the traffic towards you. Not much in the immediate vicinity other than a garage, so got some water and munchies for the train, nothing like the selection available from garages in England which seem to be like mini supermarkets nowadays, but experiencing the retail choice of different countries is all part of the fun of travelling I guess. Not that I saw it like that at the time, could have done with a better selection of snacks to compensate for the basic choice on the train.

As Winnipeg is an hour long stop where they change the crew and refuel, they make the passengers queue up to re-board, treating new and existing passengers the same, except that those in Silver and Blue classes (those with beds basically) get to board ahead of those of us in Comfort class (without beds). Bit of a pain but after a short delay we were back on the train and moving again, and I got a glimpse of the Radisson hotel where I'd stayed at previously. With this being a whole day on the train and another night ahead of us, I just wanted to get going, admire the scenery before crashing out, but no, VIA Rail had other ideas. After we crossed the bridge over the Red River the train reversed back over it and into the station again, apparently to add another carriage to the train. By now I was thinking it would have been good to have stopped in Winnipeg for a couple of nights, it's the halfway point between Jasper and Toronto, and it would be good to expand on what I saw last time. Still, maybe next time, and like I say we were half way now, and heading towards Ontario and the Canadian Shield.

Within an hour or so of leaving Winnipeg the scenery became much more typical of that associated with the Canadian Shield, as the prairies turned to forests, then the first hills we'd seen for nearly 24 hours of travelling, then lots of bare bedrock and lakes. Last time I'd been there on the train it was early spring, much of it still frozen in ice and snow, and looking very bleak. This time it was a complete contrast, with the mixed trees putting on a fine autumnal display of green, yellow, red, gold, orange and anything in between, with the added bonus of seeing water rather than ice. The scenery here reminded me somewhat of parts of Royal Deeside in Scotland, especially from Aboyne to Braemar, and is probably quite an underrated part of Canada among foreign visitors who focus more on the Rockies. I think rural Ontario, which we entered in the late afternoon thus moving onto Eastern Time, is very popular with Canadians and Americans living in the big cities of the east. Having said that, we'd only just entered Ontario and the province is huge, and we had another day of travel ahead of us yet.

It was nice though to have more interesting scenery to take in, no mountains towering overhead but colourful trees, bedrock and loose rocks, lakes, lakes, and more lakes. So many lakes! The province of Ontario is home to 20% of the world's fresh water, and as you pass through by train you begin to comprehend that statistic. And just to add another interesting fact, about 8% of Canada's territory is covered by lakes, giving it more lake area than anywhere else in the world. From what I've seen Ontario makes a big contribution to that, and it certainly makes the long train ride more enjoyable.

We arrived in Sioux Lookout at around 7pm, just as it was getting dark, and with it being another half hour stop it was a final chance to stretch our legs before settling down for the night. Sioux Lookout is a small town of about 5000 people with no large settlements nearby, but as we pulled in there I thought that it would be a good place to stay one summer and enjoy the surrounding lakes. A few passengers left the train there and a few new ones got on, and the best thing about that stop was that they must have made an adjustment to the undercarriage or whatever it's called on a train, because after that there was no more grinding squeaking noise! Fantastic! With the thought that we'd be in the pub in Toronto in 24 hours, we crashed out around 9pm. I slept well but couldn't get as comfortable as the previous night, having to adjust the leg rest a few times, but other than a few nearby passenger changes in the middle of the night in the middle of nowhere, there was nothing to keep me awake.

Chapter 3 – Ontario

Monday 1st October 2007

I woke up at around 9am and went for wash, cup of tea, and sat in the cafe car for a bit to charge up my MP3 player. We were well and truly in rural central Ontario now, and it seemed to be full of tiny stops in the middle of nowhere, with such delightful names as Oba, Elsas, Folyet and Gogma. There would be trees for miles and miles, then three of four houses and someone gets off. I guess in such remote places the train is vital. We also seemed to stop a lot for the CN freight trains, stopping for 20 minutes for one train to go past that morning. We decided to have lunch in the restaurant, which in contrast to last time is set up for Comfort class passengers in part of the buffet car, the same part where we'd played games and watched videos on the previous trip. Still, it was nice to sit at a table and eat lunch, both of us having the bison cheeseburger and salad, with a couple of beers to wash it down with, all very tasty and with a fine view of remote forest to keep an eye on.

The scenery had become a slightly less rocky and open than what we'd seen on the previous afternoon and evening, but there were still beautiful areas of lakes and rivers, surrounded by trees and rocky outcrops. We arrived in Capreol sometime after 3pm, running about three hours late, and with it being a 20 minute stop we got off to stretch our legs. The thing that stuck me was the heat, it wasn't sunny but the temperature was noticeably warmer than experienced the previous day in Winnipeg or Sioux Lookout, and that was a sign of things to come. We had a brief chat with a woman travelling with her young son, then the conductors asked if we would mind changing seats so that a group of 45 people could all sit on the same carriage. We didn't mind so got out bags and got the last two pairs of seats on one side at the end of the next carriage, opposite the seat where the two female conductors were sitting, and right next to the cafe car.

Once we got going again I sat next door to charge up my MP3 player a bit more, and had a chat with a girl from Switzerland who was travelling across Canada after finishing her studies there, and a lad from Washago, the last stop before Toronto. She had the same Trans-Canada Rail Guide book as me, except hers was the updated version. With us sitting opposite the two conductors it gave us a chance to talk to them about the journey which was interesting. They said that they work 12 days in a month, 4 trips between Toronto and Winnipeg, where they both live, or sometimes they do the Winnipeg to Vancouver part of the journey, and occasionally the Winnipeg to Churchill trip, so plenty of variety. I asked about games and videos they had on the previous trip, in the part of the buffet car where we'd just eaten, and they said that as we were in the peak season (1 June to 15 October) that part of the buffet car was used as the Comfort Class restaurant, with there being an extra carriage for Comfort class passengers in the off-peak season providing a more comfortable restaurant area.

When we were about 15 minutes past Sudbury we finally saw what we'd been waiting for, thanks to the driver radioing the train crew to say that there were a couple of black bears on the right hand side of the train. We saw them clearly, a black bear and cub running away from the train, and it was actually quite a thrill to get a clear and more prolonged view of a couple of bears. The scenery became rockier for a while, no more conifer trees; instead all thin birch type trees, then more mixed woodland with a few lakes and rivers to open up the view. As it got dark around 7pm the three hour delay, which hadn't been made up, began to kick in. We should have been in Toronto at 8pm but weren't expected until nearly 11pm, so with no view to look at and nearly 53 hours of train travel behind us, being sat on the train got a bit frustrating. I suppose 3 hours on top of 53 isn't that much when you look at the whole journey, but it felt like it at the time.

Eventually we got into the suburbs of Toronto, and finally arrived in Toronto Union Station, after 56 hours on the train, at 10-45pm. As we got off the train I couldn't believe how warm it was. Here we were in Toronto, at nearly 11 o' clock at night, in early October, and the temperature was around 20'C. It felt like we'd just got off a plane on a Mediterranean island! After walking through the station we got a taxi up to the Days Inn, checked in, got my package from Fed-Ex, the Leafs v Sens tickets (which disappointingly were just the e-tickets which are printed off on paper by the original purchaser), and went up to the room. Last time I stayed there in the previous November I was on the 8th floor, this time it was the 17th floor and a very small room. Still, I felt a bit minging after 56 hours on the train and arriving in such heat, so both of us got showered and changed before going for some beers. It was about midnight by the time we got out, but as we walked into Hoops bar it felt good to be back.

Hoops is on the corner of Yonge and Carlton Street, about a hundred yards from the Days Inn, and is a sports bar / grill, with over a hundred TVs showing all kinds of sports, food and drink being served for about 18 hours a day, and lots of very nice waitresses. Some might say my ideal bar! The bonus was seeing Sky Sports News from the UK on the TV next to our table, so that gave us a chance to catch up with the football news back home. After a few enjoyable beers we went to the McDonalds around the corner for some food, which was full of some strange looking characters to say the least, and then back to the hotel at around 2am. I was asleep within 15 minutes of finishing my food, but was awoken by Dan saying I was snoring, who then promptly fell asleep and began snoring in the way only he can. I tried the ear plugs, tried the music, but in a room that size nothing would drown out that noise, woke him up to the claim that he wasn't snoring and I was snoring, and eventually after a bit more argument I could see that four days sharing such a small room could get a bit testing, so rather than fall out I went to reception at 4am and got my own room. With the price of the room in Toronto being about half that of any of the other hotels on the trip, this was the place where we could afford the luxury of our own room, so I thought I may as well. My new room was on the sixth floor and bigger, and was similar to the room I'd stayed in on my previous visit. Peace at last!

Tuesday 2nd October 2007

After a peaceful few hours sleep I woke up at 10am and decided to start the day off with a trip to the small gym and swimming pool, which conveniently was on the same floor as my new room. I spent a relaxing hour in there, then after receiving a text message went over to Hoops bar to meet Dan. I think both of us were feeling a bit awkward after the late night argument, but a beer and quick discussion about it soon got things back to normal, and we decided to have lunch in Hoops and a few more beers. Next it was a walk up the road to the Duke of Gloucester, where I'd had some great nights on my city break to Toronto the previous November. The Duke is a British pub run by an ex-pat couple who moved over in 1976, and I was there for their 30th anniversary bash in 2006, a great night indeed! It was quite funny walking in there again, and as I got the beers in I realised the same barmaid was serving me that was there the previous year, so had a quick chat with her.

The pub was full of people watching the UEFA Champions League (or more accurately, the 1st, 2nd, 3rd and 4th placed teams cup) game between Manchester United and Roma, which finished just as we got in, and within minutes they'd all gone. So we got our seats and I sent a video clip back to Chris to remind him of some fine drinking the year before, then I recognised a couple of other bar staff from the previous trip, the Scottish landlady and Indian barman Mahir, who were so thrilled at us breathing in the helium from the balloons on the pub's anniversary night! Always seems funny to travel such a long way after such a long time (relatively) and see the same people. The next few hours were spent drinking steadily at the Duke, sitting out on the roof top patio for most of it.

By early evening we headed back down Yonge Street, and for some reason (drink + attractive female perhaps!) we got persuaded to go into the Church of Scientology place. Here we were asked to sit down and fill in a multiple choice questionnaire, but after a few dozen questions I got bored as it reminded me too much of the type of questionnaires that I end up having to do on training courses with work, that tell you what sort of motivator or organiser you are or something. Next it was the psychology awareness place, but again I lost interest and thought "what are we doing in here?"! After some very tasty food an Egyptian cafe we went back to Hoops for some more beers, then back to the Beer Cellar pub at the hotel for the final drink. I recognised the barmaid called Mimi from my previous stay at the Days Inn, as me and Chris always chatted to her when we had a few drinks in there, so had a chat with her before going up for a peaceful night's sleep. It felt good to be back in Toronto.

Wednesday 3rd October 2007

After a late breakfast at 11am we wandered down Yonge Street having decided to get the city tour bus, seeing as we'd enjoyed the Vancouver tour so much and found it a good way to see more of the city, especially with the weather being so good. It was a bit cloudy but fairly warm, with the temperature in the late teens centigrade. After a short wait we got on the yellow open top double-decker bus at Yonge-Dundas Square, getting seats on the top deck, ready for a couple of hours of sightseeing. We headed north back up Yonge Street to start with, past Carlton Street where the Days Inn is, past Hoops, the Scientology place and the Duke of Gloucester, before turning into Yorkville Avenue and the Bloor-Yorkville district, a fairly high class shopping area where I'd walked through on my previous trip to Toronto.

We then headed north up to Casa Loma (Spanish for Hill House), a small castle built in 1911-14, being the former home of financier Sir Henry Mill Pellatt. He lived there for about ten years, before it became a hotel which ultimately failed, and the castle is now owned by the City of Toronto and is a major tourist attraction. At the time we drove past there though, the place was closed for visitors as they were filming a movie there, which I later found out to be 'Twitches Too' starring no one I've heard of! Looks like quite an interesting place for a future visit, and it contains the Regimental Museum of The Queen's Own Rifles of Canada.

After the excitement of seeing a 'movie' in production, we headed back downtown, past the Ontario parliament building, to the Toronto Entertainment District, which is a large part of the downtown area and is generally bounded by the Financial District to the east, Queen Street West to the north, Spadina Avenue to the west, and the Gardiner Expressway and Harbourfront to the south. The area consists of a wide range of business, arts, sports, entertainment, nightlife and media, and seemed to be undergoing quite a bit of redevelopment work with various construction sites and new buildings going up.

The bus then took us down to the shorefront, past the Air Canada Centre, home of the mighty (maybe one day once again!) Toronto Maple Leafs, and also the Toronto Raptors basketball team, before heading out to the Distillery District. This is part of the city I was unfamiliar with, and is a historic and entertainment district located east of the downtown area, containing numerous shops, cafes and restaurants within heritage buildings of the former Gooderham and Worts Distillery. Along Front Street East we passed a fantastic piece of artwork, a 180 foot long mural depicting Toronto's history from 1793-1993, commissioned by the Toronto Sun as part of the city's bicentennial celebrations in 1993. It depicts everything from the early settlers and troops, the railway, world wars, hockey, fashion, and modern day transportation.

We then headed back along to Yonge Street and back up to Yonge-Dundas Square to complete the tour. All in all a very enjoyable tour, the tour guide Jessie was very informative and charismatic, ideal for the job, and the weather remained fine throughout. I'd never given much thought to tour buses in the past but after the experience of Vancouver and now Toronto, we decided we just had to so the same in New York. So long as the weather is fine, sitting on an open bus gives you a great chance to travel through the city, seeing the sights and hearing the sounds, so much more so than in a closed vehicle. Plus the tour buses take you to the less obvious places in a city, help you with your orientation of where you are, and of course you have the knowledge and entertainment of the tour guide.

After the bus tour we walked through the Eaton Centre, where I'd bought a few things on my two previous visits to Toronto, but neither of us were that bothered about buying anything so didn't spend much time in there. The big event of the day was the NHL match between the Toronto Maple Leafs and the Ottawa Senators, dubbed the 'Battle of Ontario', but with that being a few hours away we went for a beer in the Irish Embassy pub on Yong Street, where me and Chris had been for a beer on that wet Saturday night in 2005, before going to the Hockey Hall of Fame museum, where I'd been on my previous visit. The Hockey Hall of Fame was established in 1961 on the grounds of the Canadian National Exhibition in Toronto, before moving to its current location on Yonge Street in 1993, and is a shrine to legendary hockey players, managers, broadcasters, writers and referees.

Its natural focus is the National Hockey League, but it also covers other leagues around the world and has a detailed history of the development of the game. The highlight for me is where you can take shots with a hockey stick using plastic pucks against a video goalkeeper, who somehow saves most shots (I scored 0/5, Dan score 1/5), and even better was being in goal and stopping shots from a video on the wall in front with plastic pucks being shot out of one of the slots in the wall, where I saved 4/5. There's also the chance to commentate on selected hockey plays in the media section, which was fun, and I chose to commentate in the style of a 1950's football commentator.

The last must do thing at the Hockey Hall of Fame was to see the Stanley Cup, the ultimate prize in professional hockey, awarded to the winners of the NHL post-season play-offs, which unfortunately the Toronto Maple Leafs haven't won since 1967. This lack of success makes me following the Leafs all too similar to following Darlington and England at football! With the museum closing at 5pm and us arriving at the hall where the trophy is kept just before 5pm, the security guard initially turned us away but some pleading along the lines of "just one minute" and "we've come all the way from England to see this" meant we had a couple of minutes to see the trophy and take a photo.

Once we'd finished at the Hockey Hall of Fame, we went across to Shopsy's Bar on Yonge Street for some pre-hockey beers, which was quite nice chilling out in the late afternoon autumnal sunshine, sampling the pre-match atmosphere. The game was due to start at 7pm so we went down to the Air Canada Centre about half an hour before that, a short walk down Bay Street and under the Gardiner Expressway. It felt good to be back at the ACC having attended my first game there the previous November, a game in which the Leafs beat New York Islanders 4-2. With me being used to watching the games on TV in the early hours, it was good to be there watching the game at local time. Added to that was the opposition being the Ottawa Senators, and also it was the first game of the regular NHL season.

The Air Canada Centre has a capacity of 18,800, and was built in 1999 to replace the Maple Leaf Gardens (next door to our hotel on Carlton Street), which had been the home of the Leafs since 1931. Most of the games are officially a sell out, but this is because of season ticket sales, many of which are corporate sales, creating a huge black market for tickets. It's easy enough to get a ticket for a Leafs game so long as you are prepared to pay well over face value, and that's what we did. We paid the equivalent of about £105 for our tickets for the Sens game, which was about four times the face value, but when you travel all that way to see one or two games in a season, the additional cost of a Leafs ticket is all part of the expense, and an essential one for me. Thing is, our tickets were for the back of our block, and when we got there we found that we didn't have seats, our tickets were for the standing area, a small space for one row of people behind all of the seats. Oh well, we were there and had a good view of the ice, and with our beers in hand were all set to see the start of the NHL 2007-08 season for the mighty Toronto Maple Leafs.

Before the game started we were entertained by a Highland pipe band playing The Maple Leaf Forever, followed by the singing of O Canada, and then we were down to business. The game itself was quite entertaining, with two fights breaking out and the score going (Toronto first) 0-1, 1-1, 2-1, 2-2, 3-2, and with less than five minutes left I thought I'd continue my record of seeing the Leafs win every game attended. But with three minutes left the Sens tied the game at 3-3, and then promptly won the game 3-4 in overtime. I was gutted. Devastated in fact. So close to seeing another Leafs win and starting the season with 2 points, but we were robbed at the end. After leaving the ACC we got a taxi back up to the hotel, and went for a drink at Mick E Flynns opposite the Maple Leafs Gardens. Quite a lively pub and was it was nice sat at a table out the front, talking about the game and plans for the next few days, before heading back to the hotel bar for a final beer for the night. Mimi, the barmaid I recognised from my previous stay at the Carlton Inn, was working again, so I had a chat with her before retiring at about 1am.

Thursday 4th October 2007

Thursday would be our final day in Toronto, with the plan being to go up the CN Tower and then watch the MLS game between Toronto FC and New York Red Bulls in the evening. After breakfast at 10am, we got on the tour bus again seeing as we had a two day pass for it, and we had plenty of time to kill. The weather was very cloudy downtown but the sun was gradually forcing its way through, although even by the time we got off the bus near the CN Tower, it was still buried in the low lying clouds so we went for a coffee nearby before heading over to the tower. Seeing as it was still cloudy around the observation deck, but slowly clearing, we decided to buy the full ticket which included a short film and a simulator ride. The film about the towers construction in the early 1970s was quite interesting, but the simulator was a right load of rubbish, loads of build up to a some story where the Himalayas have been turned into a forest, and then the simulator video takes you through the process of a log going through a sawmill in the mountains. Bizarre!

It killed time though, and by the time we were done there and ready for the lift, the cloud has cleared from the top of the tower so we could look forward to some fine views. Unlike my previous two visits to the tower, the lift we took was on the lakeside of the tower which gives a different perspective but still the same amazing feeling of ascending 1100 feet in just under a minute. When we got to the main level we went straight to the second lift to take us up to the Skypod, which, at the time of visiting, was the world's highest observation deck at 1465 feet.

Although the clouds had gone from around the tower and the city, they still covered Lake Ontario right up to the shoreline, which made for some interesting photographs. The actual observation area of the Skypod is very small, and would probably take no more than 20 seconds to walk round without stopping to admire the views. It's a very eerie experience to lean over the metal barrier and look down over the sloped glass with nothing in between that and the roof of the main level. With the sun shining through and the small Skypod level being fully enclosed, it became very hot in there, like a greenhouse, so once we'd taken in the views and plenty of photos, we took the lift back down to the main level, first to cool off in the outside caged area where the wind at 1100 feet is very refreshing, then to have a beer after first walking around on the glass floor.

It was very relaxing being sat the café area of the CN Towers' main observation deck, supping a cool beer, and looking down at the city below. A complete contrast to the view at Whistlers Mountain the week before, and the outside temperature was more like 22'C than 2'C. The main focus is the skyscrapers of the business district of downtown, with smaller but still large buildings flowing outwards to the suburbs of the Greater Toronto Area, then there's Union Station below next to the Air Canada Centre, the Gardiner Expressway with all its lanes of traffic, and then the cloud covered Lake Ontario. All that hustle and bustle yet it all seemed so peaceful from up there.

Some lads sat near us in the cafe were wearing New York Red Bulls shirts, not from New York though, they all had English accents, presumably on holiday and going to the game. As I'd brought my Darlo flag over with me to take to the match, but I'd left it at the hotel, we left the CN Tower after a couple of beers and got a taxi back to the hotel, where after sorting out a problem with my room key, I got the flag and we went over to Hoops bar for pre-match beer and pizza. Even though it was early October it was still warm so neither of us bother taking jackets, despite the stadium being mostly uncovered. I had a rough idea where the stadium was having looked at maps, and it was a good 2-3 miles from where we were, so the easiest option was to get a taxi from outside the bar on Yonge Street. Once on the way the small number of beers went straight through Dan and he became rather agitated at the slightest delay with the traffic, due to a strong need to go somewhere! After some 20 minutes of him offering to drive other people's vehicles out of the way and suggesting we should stop so he could find somewhere to relieve himself, we finally arrived at the stadium where he promptly took care of his rather urgent business once through the turnstiles!

The concourse under the stands is caged in rather than walled in, and has snack bars after drinks bars all the way along, and once we got some beers in, which in North America can be taken into the stands, we went to find our seats. First thing to do though was to put up my 6x3 feet "Darlington FC" St George's flag, finding a nice place on the barriers at the front of the seating. I'd done the same at another non-Darlo / non-England match in Stavanger in 2005, and made for a good photo opportunity for the Darlo Uncovered fans' website 'Around the World' feature. Our seats were right at the back of the stand, which has no roof and no back wall, just a poled fence, and by now it was cooling down, so as nice as it was to sit in a stadium with a view of the CN Tower behind, it was getting quite cold being sat there. Only one thing for it…drink! We took advantage of the facilities and beckoned a beer seller to walk all the way to the back of the stand and sell us some beer, fantastic service and worth the $2 dollar tip!

Once the game was underway, after the American and Canadian national anthems, it was quite entertaining and Edu giving Toronto a 1-0 half time lead. The stand opposite was the main stand and the only one with a roof, albeit only covering a small part of the stand below, to our left, at the other end of the stadium, was the stand allocated for the singers, and to the right there is a spacious area with just a few rows of seats and a bar behind. I couldn't help noticing the amount of food people were getting, the stadium had plenty of empty seats at kick off but after half an hour the place was just about full, once everyone had got their food from the huge selection along the concourse down below. At half time it was time for more beers and we posed for more photos by the flag, at which point the four English New York fans we'd seen earlier started talking to us. They were all employed by the New York Red Bulls football club so had free tickets, and they supported a combination of West Ham, Newcastle and Swansea, with two of them being from Bishop Auckland in County Durham, not far from Darlington.

They said that they has a couple of spare tickets for seats next to them we could have for nothing, so rather than freeze at the back of the stand we joined them about halfway down the stand, after asking some locals to move who had sat in their spare seats. It seemed they had been getting some stick off these two locals so were quite pleased to have a couple of big English lads to take the place of the two Italian originating locals, one of whom was a bit cocky but just got laughed at, no need to be getting into trouble over there! There was some banter with the home fans due to the four of them wearing New York shirts, all good natured stuff, I was supporting Toronto although nowhere near as passionately as with the Toronto Maple Leafs, so when an own goal put Toronto 2-0 up I cheered and sang "you're not singing any more" at the four of them, which no doubt confused the home fans! A late Red Bulls goal made it 2-1 but that was the final score, and the Red Bulls fans said they'd arranged to meet some Toronto fans for a drink, so once we'd got the flag and all met up, about a dozen of us walked to Shoeless Joes' bar about a mile away. It was a good laugh walking down there, singing numerous football songs relating to Toronto, New York, England, Darlington, West Ham, Swansea and Newcastle, including a fine rendition of "let's all have a disco" as we walked past the subway station!

The pub itself was packed full of TFC fans which made the sight of four NYRB fans the cue for singing various songs taking the mick out of them. I caught the end of the Leafs game on TV, which they predictably lost, and got talking to a nice girl called Katie who'd been at the match, telling her about Darlington FC and the flag which we got a picture with. All in all a good couple of hours in there, but with the knowledge that we had to leave the hotel at 7-30am to get the train to New York, we left the pub around 11-30 and got a taxi to Hoops bar near the hotel, after getting phone numbers from Katie and one of the New York fans, the latter to hopefully meet up with on the Saturday in New York to watch the rugby with, England v Australia in the World Cup Quarter Final. We maybe should have stayed around in Shoeless Joes as it was a good laugh, but I didn't want to be too rough for the train in the morning, so after one drink in Hoops I went back to the hotel, whilst Dan stayed out for a bit longer.

Friday 5th October 2007

With the train to New York due to leave at 8-30am, we were up early and got a taxi from outside the hotel at 7-30am, both feeling quite rough from the previous day's drinking. As the taxi took us down to the station I was thinking about the time spent in Toronto, as well as the two previous visits, and had a feeling I'd be going back to what was becoming a familiar city in the not too distant future. Once at the station we had to queue for about 20 minutes before being allowed onto the platform to board the train, not what we needed with hangovers like we had! We sat at double seats opposite each other, and I think Dan was a little worse for wear than me due to staying out a bit longer, as he was soon asleep and unfortunately snoring, much to the dislike of fellow passengers! I put my headphones on and admired the view, admittedly feeling a little nauseous at times due to the hangover. I'd travelled the first part of the journey before, when me and Chris got the train to Niagara Falls and Hamilton in 2005, so parts of the scenery looked familiar, including the rather barren looking station of Aldershot where we waited for the train on the way back from Hamilton. Beyond that it would all be new, and although it was a long journey and I was suffering, I was looking forward to the journey across the border, into New York State, and down to New York City.

Chapter Four – New York

We arrived at Niagara Falls at 10-45am, crossed the bridge over the river which provided some fine photo opportunities, and travelled another mile or so to stop at the railway border crossing. We had entered the United States of America, and within minutes the border guards were on the train. All US and Canadian citizens just had to show their passports, but everyone else had to hand in their passports and disembark when told to do so, and not move around the train until then. It all sounded quite strict but the guard who was doing the talking was a right laugh, and when he collected my passport and then Dan's he said "are you two brothers?". "Yeah", I replied. "Are you guys getting along? Anything to say?". I couldn't resist, "yeah, stop snoring!", which was met with someone else saying "yeah!". All quite amusing, and soon about a dozen of us were told to get off the train and follow the guards into the small customs room. We filled in the usual visa waiver card, had our photos and finger prints taken, paid the $6 entry fee, passports stamped and were then free to go back to the train.

Once the train was formally cleared of customs, we had about 20 minutes to get off the train at the other side, stretch our legs and get some fresh air. By now it was feeling quite warm, hangovers starting to wear off, but we still had another 9 hours to go. We were soon on our way again, and as the remainder of the epic journey is in the USA, it's time for my history of America in a nutshell, as I did for Canada in the introduction to part one of this book! 'America' was 'discovered' by Christopher Columbus in 1492, although had been settled thousands of years before as Canada had, and these indigenous peoples were happy living all over the continent before the appearance of 'the white man'. Initially, European colonisation began with the Spanish in the south and the British in the north east, with the French settling a bit in the south to add to their colonies in Canada. Most of the settlers got along just fine with the locals, with many exceptions, especially in the south where for example the Spanish completely wiped out the Lucayan people of the Bahamas.

Eventually the British colonies numbered thirteen, from Maine in the north to Georgia in the south, Illinois in the west to New York in the east. Due to the ancient tradition of the British and French being at war with each other, hostilities broke out in 1756 and spanned across three continents, Europe, North America and Asia, in what became known as the Seven Years War, which lasted for, yep, you guessed it, seven years. Other European nations were involved due to various alliances, but most of the fighting was in North America and also involved various native tribes on both sides. The colonists of the British Thirteen colonies remained loyal to The Crown, or defended their new homeland depending on your point of view, and fought against the French. Much of the earlier fighting went the way of the French, but eventually with more British troops arriving and with them and their colonial colleagues adapting tactics and learning from the natives, the tide was turned and the French were given a jolly good thrashing, including the aforementioned battle at Quebec.

After the Seven Years War, greed by both the colonials and their masters from the mother country led to conflict and the settlers of the Thirteen Colonies, or some of them, declared independence in 1776. His Majesty King George III was having none of it, resulting in several years of war in which British forces actually won most of the battles, but not the decisive ones and eventually lost the war thanks to our old enemies the French and Spanish helping out the Americans, who also dealt rather harshly with those who remained loyal to the Crown. When Britain fought the Peninsula War with the French (1808-14) the Americans weren't too pleased with the trade restrictions imposed upon them by the British aimed to hamper the French war effort, so used it as an excuse to have a pop at Canada, which since the Revolutionary War had seen a large influx of Loyalist immigrants from the former Thirteen Colonies. Although the Americans took and burned much of York (now Toronto), they didn't get much further, and once the British beat the French in the Peninsula War, reinforcements arrived and the British landed at Washington DC and set fire to the White House. The Americans successfully defended Baltimore which became the source of their national anthem, the Star Spangled Banner, and they defended New Orleans, but they couldn't take Canada and with the treaty of Ghent taking effect in February 1815, two months after being signed, all territories were returned to their previous owners and the Brits and Yanks have since lived happily ever after. A score draw in my books!

The United States of America then expanded through a mixture of conquest, purchase, annexation and settlement, mainly to the west, but also to the south (Florida), far north west (Alaska) and far west (Hawaii). The southern states and the northern states then decided they didn't like each other and eleven southern states declared independence from the United States of America to form the Confederate States of America, which led to a very divisive civil war from 1861-1865 in which over 600,000 soldiers died. The north won the civil war, ending slavery and giving freedom to the millions of mainly African slaves that had been brought there for generations. All this expansion meant that the native Americans were moved out of their homelands, starved and slaughtered all over the continent, all so the 'the white man' could keep on settling new land and making more money, although this didn't come easy for the Americans whose military suffered notable defeats culminating in the infamous Battle of the Little Bighorn in 1876.

As the country expanded the Wild West became less wild, more and more immigrants came to America from all over the world but especially Europe, and the USA became a prosperous yet slightly isolationist country. When the First World War started in 1914, it seemed a world away to Americans, however they joined the Allies in 1917 and helped to defeat the Germans in 1918. When the Second World War started in 1939, the US was reluctant to get involved until the Japanese bombed the American fleet at Pearl Harbour in Hawaii, after which they thankfully joined the British Empire, Soviet Union, and many countries around the world in defeating the Axis forces of Germany, Japan and Italy. The 'West' then fell out with the 'East' which led to the Cold War which fortunately never resulted in military conflict, and the USA was left at the end of the 20th century as the richest and most powerful country on the planet. And there, in a nutshell, is my history of the United States of America! Despite a touch of tongue in cheek criticism there, I'll say now that I like America and its people, and I thoroughly enjoy visiting there, and was certainly looking forward to my time in New York and Boston. So, after that little interlude, it's back to the journey!

The first stop was Buffalo, the first major city over the border where a few more passengers embarked, and then Rochester, or Raaachester to Americans, where a number of students got on the train, presumably going home for the weekend. It was clearly very hot outside and the temperature inside was no better due to the air conditioning on our carriage being on the blink, although it wasn't much better in the adjoining carriages which were just as packed as ours, so we didn't bother moving. It was nice taking in the scenery though, and as we headed through New York State I sometimes thought about the troops that would have been fighting their way through the dense forest of the New World during the Seven Years War and Revolutionary War, as the land would have been mostly wilderness back in those days. We were soon passing through Rotterdam and Amsterdam, completely unlike their Dutch namesakes but in quite scenic surroundings, and then on to Albany, the capital of New York State. The train had longer stop at Albany, giving us a chance to stretch our legs and get some fresh air, and I sent a text message to Mel, who I'd met up with in New York in 2005 at the end of their round the world trip, as his brother in law lives in Albany.

Quite a few passengers left the train at Albany, including the girl who'd been sat next to me for a while, and fewer passengers got on the train so there was more room to spread out. Albany marked a change in direction as we'd been mainly heading east to get there, but we were now heading south to New York City and into the darkness of the October evening. The next few hours of travelling through the darkness were reminiscent of the last few hours before Toronto. We were tired from the journey, warm, and eagerly anticipating arrival in a large and exciting city. As we pulled into Yonkers, north of New York, we knew there wasn't far to go, and soon we were alongside the Hudson River and into Manhattan itself, where the train went underground and into our destination, Penn Station. Finally, at about 10pm, after over 13 hours on the train that was too hot, we'd arrived in New York, which was also too hot! It felt even hotter than Toronto when we arrived there, as hot as when I flew to Rhodes in 2003 arriving to humid heat at 3am.

Despite the heat it was a buzz to be in New York with all the hustle and bustle, and Dan was clearly thrilled to be there despite the heat and the long journey. After waiting about 10 minutes in the taxi rank we were on our way to the Pod Hotel, on East 53rd and 2nd Avenue, which the driver seemed to have trouble understanding despite the clear directions. We soon got there though without any detour, and once checked in went to our room to get sorted. By now it was 11pm, and after the long day we were in need of a few beers and a short walk to check out the locality of the hotel. The room itself was very small, but absolutely brilliant. I'd read about the hotel on the internet before booking, and it had been recently refurbished. Our room had a bunk bed, each bunk having its own LCD TV, a sink, table, chair, and some cupboard space. The bathrooms were shared with four on each floor, but they were all immaculately clean and each room had a light indicator for the bathrooms to show when they were free.

We didn't know much about the immediate locality around the hotel and decided to head left towards 3rd Avenue, which had a few shops but we couldn't see any bars until we found a TGI Fridays on Lexington Avenue, another block along from 3rd Avenue. We decided to go in there for some beers and a bite to eat, it was nothing special and they played rap music which I don't particularly like, but we were just enjoying the buzz of being in New York and looking forward to a few days there. The beer was going down well after the long day on the train as well! We were quite tired though and headed back to the hotel after midnight, where I found that a combination of being in a bunk bed and having our own TVs reduced the audibility of my brother's snoring a somewhat! Still needed the ear plugs eventually though and got a good night's sleep!

Saturday 6th October 2007

The day started with the both bad news and good news. The bad news was that we'd missed seeing the England v Australia rugby World Cup game, which we'd assumed was an evening kick off over in France, meaning an afternoon in the pub to watch it, but it actually started at 3pm French time so 9am New York time, and as we were just about ready to leave the hotel room we got the score via a text message. That was the good news – England won 12-10 to reach the World Cup Semi-Finals, quite a surprise given the bad start to the tournament and the ongoing 'rebuilding' since winning the cup in 2003.

Before leaving the hotel we decided to go up to the 14th floor where there was access to the roof, which has a small wooden patio area and provides a reasonable view of the surrounding area. I say reasonable because although this was the top of a 14 storey building, which in most towns in the UK would provide a view for miles, this was New York, and the building was dwarfed by many of the surrounding buildings, so we couldn't actually see that far. It was great though, looking down at the drop to the ground, looking around to similar sized buildings, and looking up to those that towered above. It was also very hot, not a cloud in the sky and the temperature must have been around 30'C, with the forecast on my new favourite TV station, The Weather Channel, predicting more of the same for the rest of our time in the city.

After browsing the tourist leaflets in the hotel reception we decided to walk up to 64th & 5th to get a tour bus, with the weather being ideal for it. Navigation around much of Manhattan is quite easy due to its grid system, with the numbered streets going up from Downtown, and the avenues going up from the east side of the island. Whenever you go somewhere in New York, especially in a taxi, you should know both the street it's on and the nearest one which crosses it. Not all are numbered, but you should still know the nearest intersection. Our walk to 64th Street & 5th Avenue was less than a mile but very hot, and took us to the side of Central Park where we waited for a tour bus to turn up. We didn't have to wait too long, and although the bus was quite full, the tour guide said that the current tour ended just around the corner so the other passengers would be disembarking giving us the chance to sit upstairs on the open top deck. Once on 7th Avenue it was all change and we had the pick of the seats upstairs, so sat at the back, ready for a couple of hours of sightseeing.

With the temperature being so high and there being practically no wind, it was such a relief when the bus started moving and we had the rush of air to cool us down, albeit intermittent movement due to the New York traffic. The ticket we'd bought was valid for three days and included all of the routes – the downtown loop, the uptown loop, the Brooklyn loop and the night time loop, costing about $60 or just £30 with the exchange rates at the time, which offered great value for money. The downtown loop that we'd just started took us down the middle of Manhattan along 7th Avenue, around Madison Square Gardens where ice hockey, boxing and other sports take place, past the Empire State Building and Flat Iron Building, through Greenwich Village and Soho, and right down to the southern tip of Manhattan at Battery Park, an area I'd walked around 22 months previous when I first visited New York.

It was a very enjoyable way of the city, and credit is due to the tour guide who kept on talking despite us often being stuck in traffic, telling us about all sorts such as the water storage tanks visible on top of nearly all buildings, the construction of the Empire State Building, and how Wall

Street got its name, which was from when New York was a Dutch colony called New Amsterdam and that was its northern perimeter, marked by a wall which was strengthened over time to resist attacks by the Native Americans, New England colonists and the British, although it was never actually used for its defensive purposes.

From there the bus headed up the east side of Manhattan, past Chinatown and Little Italy, past the United Nations next to the East River, and past the Rockefeller Centre where we decided to get off the bus. After a brief look around the shops, where Dan bought some shorts, we had a late lunch at the Morrell cafe, sitting outside in the shade and watching the world go by, including some plain clothed policemen bringing down a criminal of some description, which was quite entertaining (bringing down as in pulling them to the ground, not shooting them!). Next on the agenda was the Rockefeller Centre, outside which is a very picturesque open air ice rink, surrounded by flags from around the world and a gold statue. I'd seen this ice rink before, but that was at New Year with temperatures around zero, but I was amazed to see the ice there in these temperatures of over 30'C, although there seemed to be a lot of surface water and there weren't many people skating.

Once inside the Rockefeller we bought our tickets for 'Top of the Rock' or 'Taaap of the Raaack', and were pleased to see that the queues were quite small, certainly compared to the Empire State Building I'd been to on my previous visit. On the way there I had to make a comment about the directions we'd been given – "down that corridor and make a left", which, as we walked alongside a glass wall to our left would mean smashing it down, "can't we just *take* a left turn instead of *making* one" I said to Dan. Just another amusing observation about the American use of the English language! We were guided into a room where a video about the building was shown for five minutes or so, before we joined the queue for the lift. After a short wait we were in the lift (or elevator as they say in the USA!), and this in itself was quite good as the roof is glass and the elevator shaft (I'm learning) was full of lights of all different colours, which makes for quite a spectacular display as one ascends to the top.

Like I say I'd been up the Empire State Building on previous visit to New York, and when we reached the top of the Rockefeller Centre two things stood out which perhaps offer a better view. Firstly there is a clear view of Central Park, where one can really appreciate the vastness of the park and see it in contrast to Manhattan Island. Secondly, the view of downtown includes the Empire State Building, providing the opportunity to take some quite iconic photos. It's not as high as the Empire State Building but certainly gives a great view all around, and it's not as crowded either. It was quite enjoyable spending time up there, admiring the view in all directions, and even cooling off slightly due to the wind at altitude (850 feet). Once we finished taking pictures and enjoying the views, we walked back to the hotel, only a few blocks away, to chill out and get changed before going out for a few beers.

Rather than going far we decided to look for bars near the hotel, this time turning right and going onto 2nd Avenue. Before we got that far we had a drink at the Montparnasse café next to the hotel, where the Stella was tasting fine and got the night in motion. When Dan went outside for a cigarette he got talking to a Glaswegian woman, who was sat outside so she could smoke and was complaining about her food, and seemed to have been drinking longer than we had to put it mildly. Nevertheless, Dan invited her to join us at the next pub, which was Jamesons on 2nd Avenue, an Irish pub with a reasonable selection of beers, although unfortunately not any fine Canadian ales such as Alexander Keiths. We were in quite a good location there, sat by the open window overlooking 2nd Avenue, but soon it was time to move on and leave the slightly inebriated Glaswegian.

The next pub was Opal, just up the road, which was quite a smart bar full of well dressed professional type people, we got talking to a few of them, had quite a few drinks in there, and then moved on to the final bar of the night, TJ Whitneys, around the corner from Opel. We sat at the bar in this bar, which was much quieter, had a few beers and finished off with some spirits, before going for some pizza from a nearby snack van, which we took back to the hotel. All in all a good Saturday night, not too drunk but we'd had a few and at least found a few more bars near to the hotel.

Sunday 7th October 2007

We had a late start to the day due to the beers the night before, and the plan was to go down to the Staten Island ferry to get a view of the Statue of Liberty, and then make further use of the three day bus tickets we'd bought. The Staten Island ferry is a free service which goes from the southern end of Manhattan Island to Staten Island, another of the five Boroughs of New York, the others being Brooklyn, Queens and The Bronx. The ferry is a great way to get a closer look at the Statue of Liberty, as well as getting to experience the waterways around New York and visit another Borough. We got a taxi down there, which took us down the east side of Manhattan past some of the places we'd been through on the bus during the previous afternoon.

Once we arrived at the ferry terminal we had a short wait along with hundreds of other passengers, as we awaited for one of the ferries to take us on the 5 mile and 25 minute journey to Staten Island. As soon as the ramp was down on the incoming ferry the incoming passengers disembarked, and then it was the time for us to board the ferry. We headed straight for the outside deck upstairs, along with many others who were eager to get a view of the Statue of Liberty. We were soon on our way, and watching the southern end of Manhattan slowly edge into the distance, which reminded me of last time I'd experienced the view, albeit from significantly higher up in a helicopter during my previous visit. Attention then turned to the Statue of Liberty, with the ferry passing about half a mile away, providing plenty of good photo opportunities. It was certainly a good way to clear a hangover, getting the fresh air on deck and admiring the scenery of New York and New Jersey. We hadn't researched Staten Island so planned on coming straight back, and once docked at the other side all passengers had to disembark and queue up with other passengers waiting for the Manhattan bound ferry, although due to the volume of passengers already waiting we'd have to wait for the next one.

As we were sat waiting for another ferry to arrive my phone rang, but as it just said "call" rather than the name of the person calling from my phone book, I ignored it as I thought it would be some kind of marketing call from the UK, not something I wanted to pay international charges for. A minute later I had an answer phone message alert, and despite having not answered the phone to avoid international charges, I had to see who it was. The message was from my dad, and as soon as I heard his voice I knew what he was going to say. Our aunt Penny, my dad's sister, had been seriously ill for a few weeks with cirrhosis of the liver, and things were looking very grim before we went away. My dad confirmed my fears and said that she'd died at around 4-30pm UK time, which would have been 11-30am New York time, when we would have been in the taxi down to the ferry terminal.

I was devastated. I wanted to tell Dan but just couldn't speak. I tried taking my mind of it by thinking of other things, but as soon as I thought about telling him I choked up again, so held my tongue as I didn't want to start crying in front of hundreds of people. "I'll tell him on the ferry", I thought to myself. Once on the ferry we were on the open deck along side of the boat, and again, I struggled to get the words out despite the fresh air and the views across the water. Finally, having been silent since the phone call and as we were about to dock back at Manhattan, I told Dan that Dad had phoned, but even then he had to finish what I started trying to say, having guessed what the message was. A very difficult moment indeed, and we decided to go for a beer before phoning home. Strangely enough, the moment seems to have been immortalised for me by the making of a video slide show when I got back, as a memento of the trip, to which I used the aforementioned song Highwayman. As I finalised which photos to use and then played it back with the music, the lyrics "*and when I reach the other side, I'll find a place to rest my spirit if I can…*" are heard at the point that a couple of photos taken from the Staten Island ferry are displayed. Purely coincidental, but very poignant.

Once we left the ferry terminal we turned right and walked about half a mile up to Pier 17, taking in views of the Brooklyn, Manhattan and

Williamsburg bridges – a good way to remember which bridge is which is to think of BMW, as that gives the order the bridges are in as you head north. Pier 17 is the location of the South Street Seaport, a complex containing numerous shops, bars and restaurants, and is the docking place for water taxis and sailing ships, quite a pleasant area to spend time in. We went to the Heartland Brewery for a couple of beers, a bar I'd been to before on the other side of South Street, which runs underneath the Franklin D Roosevelt Drive elevated highway, and we sat outside there for about an hour or so, during which time we phoned home.

By late afternoon we decided to get the bus which did the Brooklyn loop, which leaves from next to Pier 17, only to be told that the Brooklyn loop had finished for the day. Instead we got the downtown loop back up to Times Square, and decided to do the night time tour later on, which crosses over into Brooklyn. First though it was time for food and beer, so we went to Charley O's on Broadway, which was only a few minutes from where we'd need to get the bus later on. It was quite busy in there, not surprising given its location one block north of Times Square, but a good meal, both of us opting for a pizza. The night tour starts from the Gray Line Visitors Centre at 47th and 8th, near Times Square, and has no stops along the way, leaving at 6pm and getting back at 8pm.

So having filled our stomachs with pizza and beer we were ready for the night tour, sitting on the open upper deck near the back. The route takes in the main sites of Manhattan, passing the Empire State Building, down to Greenwich Village, Soho, Chinatown, the Lower East Side, then over the Manhattan Bridge to Brooklyn. This included a stop along a quiet street near the East River which gave us fabulous views of Manhattan, all lit up in its night time glory, before crossing back over the Brooklyn Bridge. Manhattan, especially by night, is one of those iconic views that is seen so much in pictures and on TV, so it's great to see it first hand from the other side of the water. Once back over into Manhattan we passed through Union Square on 14th to 17th street, which is the area where I'd stayed on my first visit to New York, before getting back to Times Square around 8pm. All in all a great tour, a good way to spend a couple of hours, and we'd certainly got our money's worth from the 3 day ticket we'd bought.

Before going to New York the first time I'd looked on the internet for pubs which show English football, and found one called the Red Lion in Greenwich which looked good, although we never made it there in that trip. One of the English NYRB fans suggested the pub for the rugby, and told us it was on Thompson and Bleecker, but we didn't get up early enough for the rugby. So with the bus tour complete, we decided to get a taxi down to Greenwich to check it out. The pub itself has a bright red and yellow exterior, but inside is quite dark and is focused on providing live sport, including British football, and live music, as well as the usual North

American selection of food, with some British specialties such as shepherd's pie thrown in.

It was quite a decent pub, but after a few beers we decided to move on and try some more along Bleecker Street, the next being The Village Lantern, where we sat at the front of the pub by the open sliding doors. A good place to keep cool, watch the comings and goings, yet it wasn't too far from the bar. The next pub was the Slane, a small Irish pub which was quite well decorated, but fairly quiet. The area around Bleecker Street is quite chilled out and made a nice change from the hustle and bustle of Times Square, expanding on ones perception of New York.

Having had a few beers all evening, the pizza being several hours behind us, and our eating habits having got into a habit of a late start and late finish, we decided to go for a curry. On my previous trip I'd been to East 6th Street, which is like a smaller version of Brick Lane in London, much smaller in fact, but still containing a good selection of Indian restaurants. There was only one choice as far as I was concerned, the Gandhi where I'd been before and had a great meal. We arrived not long before closing time, but still had time to get our orders in, great food but a bit rushed due to them wanting to close. Still, good to go back there and it was a fine end to the day's proceedings. After that it was a taxi back to the Pod Hotel and time for bed, ready for our final full day in New York.

Monday 8th October 2007

Our last full day in New York, and with us having had a few beers and a curry the night before, we were up late and weren't too fussed about anything to eat. The plan was to have one last day on the tour bus, this time doing the uptown loop, and then travel around on the subway to wherever took our fancy. We walked up to Central Park around midday to get the bus, the weather was still nice and sunny, and we'd be seeing a part of town we'd not been to previously. Whilst waiting for the bus Dan got onto one of the bike taxis that were parked up next to the park, which made a good photo, but then he had trouble stopping it from rolling away until the owner came along and applied the brake! As the uptown route doesn't pass as many famous landmarks as the downtown loop, and with it being a Monday, the bus wasn't as crowded and we got seats near the back again, enjoying the warm sunshine and cooling breeze as we moved along.

The bus took us up the western side of Central Park, and the first thing of note was the apartment building outside which John Lennon was shot on 8 December 1980. I'd seen the nearby Strawberry Fields memorial to him in Central Park on my first visit to New York, and although only 7 years old at the time of his death, I distinctly remember seeing it on the news.

Furthermore I was a big Beatles fan as a child, so with a slight sense of morbid fascination, it was quite interesting to see the spot where the nutcase Mark Chapman ended his life for no reason. We then continued along the western side of Central Park, with numerous buildings be pointed out by the tour guide as being the homes of the rich and famous, we passed the Natural History Museum, which is well rated and a good excuse to go to New York again, and then up as far as the George Washington Bridge, which links Manhattan to New Jersey. We then went through Harlem, heading east, before heading down the east side of Central Park and back to our starting point. It had been good to see more of New York with the information from the tour guide to supplement the sights and sounds, but by now, having not eaten for about 15 hours, we were starving!

We walked down 7th Avenue, looking for somewhere good to eat, and eventually found Ben Ash Delicatessen. Having had no breakfast, no lunch, and a few beers the night before, everything on the menu looked good and I was ready for a good feed. The seafood platter caught my eye, although I was surprised at the variety of things listed on there, with fish, scampi, prawns, chips and many other things. It also said something about ideal for sharing, but as I was so hungry I was happy to have it all to myself. Dan went for a New York club sandwich. When the food came out I was gobsmacked at the amount of the food on my plate! The plate itself was about a foot wide, and contained enough food for three people! The menu didn't lie! I was starving though and was determined to make a good go of it, but there was no way I could eat it all, as nice as it was. I managed about two thirds of it, and was absolutely completely and utterly stuffed! I don't think I've ever been as full in my life as I was after eating that!

Once we'd finished there, feeling very bloated, we went to the Subway having decided to travel down to Coney Island, at the south end of Brooklyn. The main reason for going there was that it was where the gang came from in the 1979 film The Warriors, which I'd also bought the PS2 game for, so thought it would be good to go and visit. Once the train crossed over into Brooklyn, our fellow passengers became less tourists and more locals, and the journey to Coney Island took about half an hour, during which time our stomachs were working overtime to digest all that food from the New York deli! As we approached Coney Island it was a thrill to see the famous Wonder Wheel featured in both the Warriors film and the game, along with all the other fairground rides.

Walking out of the subway station I just had to say a line from the film – "Warriors, Warriors, come out to play", before we took turns in posing for pictures outside the station entrance! For those that haven't seen the film, it's about a small street gang who go to a big meet of New York's gangs up in Pelham, The Bronx, with the different gangs all wearing strange and distinctive outfits. One of the leaders gets shot by someone who accuses the Warriors of the shooting, and they spend the rest of the film fighting and running back to Coney Island. The other gang member who actually did the shooting turns up and is seen banging a couple of bottles together saying "Warriors, Warriors, come out to play", and then there's a lively end to the film. Quite entertaining and I'm surprised it's not been re-made in one form or another.

Coney Island used to be an island until part of the Coney Island Creek was filled in during the 1950s as part of the construction of the Belt Parkway, and it had become a popular resort for New Yorkers, reaching its peak in the earlier part of the 20th century. Since then it has seen some decline, but the impression one gets walking round is not so much one of dereliction, more one of being in a time warp. Walking along Surf Avenue and then onto the wooden promenade by the beach, past the tacky shops, hot dog stands and fairground rides, it almost feels like being in the 1960s or 70s. It was quite good though slowly walking along there, then stopping for a beer at Ruby's on the promenade, although that was a struggle due to still feeling bloated from all that food. Being at the southern tip of Brooklyn, on the Atlantic coast, gives a sense of separation from the hustle and bustle of Manhattan, and I could see why it developed as a resort over the years.

After just the one beer we decided to walk back to the subway station, on the way passing a building sized advert for Nathan's International Hot Dog Eating contest, which is held every year on the 4th July. This had a digital countdown to the next one, in 269 days, 18 hours and 1 minute, and gave the all time records – 39 hot dogs was the female record, and a staggering 66 hot dogs was the male record! All those hot dogs and buns, eaten in the space of a mere 12 minutes! I was still feeling stuffed from the food at the deli, so God knows how the competitors in the hot dog eating contest feel!

We were soon back on the subway heading back up towards Manhattan, although saw quite a surreal sight a couple of stops past Coney Island, with a large red 'W' spray painted on a wall, in the style of the 'Warriors' in the film! The subway train itself was air conditioned which made the journey much more enjoyable on such a warm day, something I'd love to see happen on the London Underground. Once back at Times Square, our digestive systems had been working hard to make room for more beer, so we went to the Hard Rock cafe, having an enjoyable drink sat at the bar. After that we had a wander around Times Square, taking photos of a beggar who was holding a sign saying "Need money to get drunk so that 2 women can take me home and molest me" before giving him a dollar each. He probably wasn't even homeless but it made us laugh.

From there the search for the amber nectar took us the nearby O'Lunney's Irish pub, a decent place on West 45th Street where we had some Stella Artois. Next it was the Perfect Pint, another Irish pub, before we got a taxi back to the hotel, although from there we went onto 2nd Avenue and went for a drink in Clancy's bar. In there, everyone was glued to the TV matching the baseball, not a game I have any interest in or understanding of, but seeing as we were in New York we wanted the New York Yankees to win. Apparently it was the deciding game in a post-season play off series, but unfortunately the Yankees lost and the pub emptied. Oh well. We stayed for another beer, before going for some pizza and taking it back to the hotel. Our time in New York had come to an end, and the next day we would be getting the train up to Boston for our last train journey of the trip.

Chapter Five - Massachusetts

Tuesday 9th October 2007

After a weekend of hot and sunny weather, the Weather Channel was forecasting cloud and lower temperatures for New York, and colder weather for Boston, which would be quite a relief after the sometimes excessive heat we'd experienced. In a way it was sad to be leaving the Pod Hotel and the delights of New York, but we had the last part of the adventure to look forward to, and for me, the first time we'd be going to a city I'd not been to before. We checked out of the hotel and got a taxi to Penn Station around 10:30am, nice and early for our train which was due to leave at 12:03pm. The train tickets has been bought over the internet but had to be collected from the station, and due to the length of the queue at the ticket office I eventually sussed out the ticket machine and collected the tickets from there.

After waiting around in the waiting area for a while, we were able to board the train and were soon on our way, leaving New York on the final train journey of the trip. The train was the Acela Express which travels from Washington DC to Boston, and included stops at Stamford and New Haven in Connecticut, Providence in Rhode Island, before reaching Boston, Massachusetts. With it having been dark when we arrived in New York, it was nice to see the scenery of the northern part of the city in daylight, watching the skyscrapers of Manhattan fade into the distance, to eventually be replaced by countryside. The route followed the coast for a while, and became very scenic as we made our way into New England, before finally arriving at Boston South Station at 3-40pm. So, after two and half weeks, 4000 miles, 4 time zones, and God knows how many beers, we'd reached the end of the line, Boston. Another trans-continental train journey had been completed, from the Pacific coast to the Atlantic coast, west to east. Before heading home though, we had a new city to explore for the next three days.

It was noticeably cooler than in New York, and as we left the station we noticed something strange. It was quiet. There was no constant drone of traffic, with the beeping of horns every few seconds. The yellow cabs had been replaced by white cabs, and were far fewer in number. As much as I enjoyed New York, my first impression of Boston was that it would be a more relaxed place to end the trip. Back home, Darlington were playing Leeds United in a cup game that was being shown live on Sky Sports, and as Fox Sports World usually show Sky's live games, I was hoping to catch the end of the match in a pub. I'd not looked up a sports bars on the internet prior to arrival, so asked a couple of newspaper vendors outside the station. "Excuse me, is there a sports bar near here?". "A whaat?" "A sports bar". "What's one of those?" "A bar that shows sport on TV. A pub showing sports." "Oh, I don't know". "Okay, thanks". After that not particularly useful conversation we decided to wander down the road to see what we could find. With us carrying rucksacks and the match being nearly over anyway (it would've been around 9pm back home), we didn't want to walk too far and went in to the Revolution Rock Bar. No Fox Sports showing football (or soccer as the locals say), but a nice enough bar to enjoy a couple of beers whilst getting score updates via text message. Darlo lost 1-0 to a late goal, so we weren't missing anything.

After a couple of beers we got a taxi to our hotel, the Constitution Inn, across the harbour in the Charlestown Navy Yard complex. It seemed a bit out of the way when we got there, but the hotel itself is great, plenty of facilities, decent sized rooms, and less than £50 each per night. I enquired on reception about a laundry service, having not had any done since Toronto, and they told me there's a self service laundrette downstairs near the gym. That gave me the chance to get some clean clothes for the last few days of the trip, and also have a quick look at the gym. Once we'd got showered, changed, and clothes washed, it was time to head out for something to eat and a drink. We weren't too fussed about going into town and the reception staff advised us of a pub called the Tavern on the water, which funnily enough, was a pub right next to the harbour.

There were some great views across the harbour of downtown Boston from there, the food was great, and the beers were good, but after a couple of hours we decided to wander around to see what else we could find having been told about a smaller Bistro bar. We finally found the Bistro, and it was much smaller and more of a restaurant than a bar, so after one beer we went to the nearby shop and bought some essentials to take back to the hotel – a bottle of rum and some snacks. That was it for the night; we'd arrived in Boston, were pleased with the hotel, had a decent meal, and were ready to explore the city the next day, after sampling the Morgan's Spiced Rum of course! Our plan for the day was to find out more about Boston's history, visiting the nearby USS Constitution and then visiting the site of the Battle of Bunkers Hill during the Revolutionary War, before resuming our usual task of sampling the local alcoholic and culinary delights.

Wednesday 10th October 2007

Boston is one of the USAs oldest cities having been established by English puritan colonists in 1630. Its growth led to it being the largest city in the American colonies before being overtaken by Philadelphia. It later became synonymous with the Revolutionary War, most famously the Boston Tea Party, when, in protest against the taxation being imposed by the British government, locals boarded a merchant ship one night and threw its cargo of tea overboard into the harbour. During the war itself the city was the scene of the Battle of Bunkers Hill in 1775, which we'd be finding out more about later.

Our first port of call, if you excuse the pun, was the USS Constitution, moored a short walk away in the Charlestown Navy Yard harbour. I was quite surprised at the security here, which was just as you'd expect at an airport, with us having to empty pockets and go through a metal detector. After a short wait we were taken round on a guided tour with about 20 people being in each tour group. The tour itself was very fascinating, providing an insight into life on a warship in the early 19th century, even if it was a ship that saw action against my fellow countrymen, which prompted me to say to Dan, in my blindly patriotic way, "I bet she wouldn't have fared so well against HMS Victory!"

The ship was launched in 1797, designed to be bigger and more heavily armed than other frigates at the time, and became famous for its exploits in the War of 1812, when it defeated five British ships and gained the nickname "Old Ironsides". This wasn't because its sides were actually made of iron, but because the southern live oak, a very dense wood, which was used for the hull at a depth of 21 inches instead of the more common 18 inches, made many of the cannon balls fired at the ship simply bounce off, apparently leading to a sailor on board shouting out "Huzzah! Her sides are made of iron!" The ship is still commissioned today and remains the oldest commissioned warship in the world, and when it's not acting as a museum in Charlestown Navy Yard, it can be seen on various public events to celebrate the history of the US Navy.

To continue on the theme of the Revolutionary War, we then walked up to the Bunkers Hill Monument which is actually sited on Breeds Hill next to Bunkers Hill, and is less than a mile from the USS Constitution. As we walked up the hill through the quiet streets, I couldn't resist playing a clip of 'The British Grenadiers' music on my phone, knowing that 232 years earlier the same music had been played in the same place to accompany British troops marching up the hill, but for us the only potential danger was the occasional traffic, rather than musket balls and cannon balls.

The Battle of Bunkers Hill is named after a hill which was the original British objective, but most of the battle took place on Breeds Hill and that's where the Bunkers Hill monument is. In 1775, prior to the Declaration of Independence in 1776 but after hostilities had broken out between the British and the United Colonies, the American forces had besieged Boston to prevent the movement of the British troops garrisoned there. This siege lasted from April 1775 until March 1776 when the British finally evacuated by sea, but in June 1775 the British had plans to occupy a couple of hills outside of the city, Bunkers Hill and Breeds Hill. Learning of this plan the Americans occupied them first and quickly built some entrenched fortifications there, as on 17 June 1775, the British attacked the colonial forces, suffering heavy losses and being repulsed on the first two attacks, but finally taking their objectives on the third assault. Although the British won the Battle of Bunkers Hill, it was at a heavy cost with 226 soldiers killed and 828 wounded, compared to 115 killed, 305 wounded and 30 captured from the defending forces. Furthermore the victory didn't do much to alleviate the siege of Boston and the British were forced to evacuate to Halifax, Nova Scotia, the following spring. From a modern perspective this shows the apparent absurdity in sending lines of men against fortified positions, but I guess that's how war was done in those days and respect to all involved, it must have been quite horrific, as are all wars.

The Bunkers Hill Monument is 221 feet high and contains 294 steps up a narrow spiral staircase, and was good exercise / bloody knackering depending on your viewpoint! It's quite a small space at the top and the windows are very narrow, but it gave a great view of the surrounding area, not quiet the CN Tower or Rockefeller but good nonetheless. After spending about 20 minutes at the top, enjoying the views and cooling off from the climb, we went back down the 294 steps, much easier than climbing although easy to get dizzy from going down so fast, and I couldn't resist playing the British Grenadiers on my phone again which echoed back up the staircase! Once back at ground level I had a conversation with the lady who worked there, as I'd recognised the painting on one of the walls downstairs, it being on the cover of a book I'd read about the war, called Redcoats and Rebels, which she'd read herself. Quite a good objective account of the war, although heavy reading at times.

There was a small museum at the foot of the grass covered area where the monument is, and this provided a further insight into the Battle of Bunkers Hill. I was particularly fascinated by the models of the battle, huge landscapes with lines of metal soldiers all over the place, helping to give some perspective of events back in 1775. There's nothing glorious in war, but both the experience of visiting the Bunkers Hill Monument and museum, and the previous visit to Fort York in Toronto, have helped give me an insight into an earlier time, trying to imagine what it was like to be stationed so far away from home, living life on the edge, either in remote conditions like in Fort York, or in bloody battle like in Boston.

Any museum that helps you understand the lives of people in the past is a good one, and although small, this museum about a battle in 1775 had achieved that. I was particularly moved by the words of William Pitt on display, who said this of the British Army in the American Revolution: "No man thinks more highly of them than I do, I love and honour the English troops, I know their virtue and their valour, I know they can achieve anything except impossibilities." Although I'm not sure what the Scottish,

Welsh and Irish troops in the army would have thought of his reference to 'English' rather than 'British' troops!

After that we got a taxi over to Cornwalls pub, a British themed pub which we'd seen on the internet, and something of a rarity in a city which prides itself so heavily on its Irish heritage and connections to the American Revolutionary War. The pub is on Beacon Street at Kenmore Square, slightly west of downtown. The interior was well decorated with paintings of Winston Churchill, Horatio Nelson and other British icons, they had a number of British type beers brewed locally, similar to the micro-brewery In Gingers Granite Brewery in Halifax two years previously. Best of all though was the menu, and after three weeks of having chips with nearly every meal, it just had to be shepherd's pie, which went down a treat.

Next stop was another British style pub, the Elephant & Castle, part of the chain which also had pubs in Toronto. I'd not been to any of their Toronto pubs, but Dan did when he's stayed out later one night. We began walking to the Elephant & Castle, along Commonwealth Avenue which seemed like a typical Boston street – wide, tree-lined, with a mixture of 19th and 20th century buildings either side, before getting a taxi that conveniently appeared just as we were wondering how far it was back into town. The Elephant & Castle was a modern, clean pub with a British theme to it, quiet when we arrived but suddenly filled up with people after finishing their day in the office. After a couple in there we moved on to JJ Foleys, an Irish pub nearby, but it took ages to find another pub.

Finally we found a pub called The Tap on Union Street, which had a good selection of pubs along it, so we made our way along there with stops at Paddy O's, the Green Dragon, and then The Point on Hanover Street. I was delighted when I walked into The Point, aged 34, to be asked for ID by the barmaid, but then the doorman said not to bother and I saw the sign saying that customers who look under 30 will be asked for ID, but it was still something! The juke box in there was good with plenty of good tunes to choose from including The Stone Roses, so we spent quite a while in there before moving on. It had been a good few hours spent drinking along Union Street, which in a way was more English in style than American, a small narrow winding street with some characteristic bars close together, but with us needing some final entertainment for the evening we decided to take up the suggestion of someone to visit the Centrefold lap dancing club! I've no idea where this was in relation to where we'd been, but after an hour or so in there, drinking rum, I'd consumed enough for the night and we got a taxi back to the hotel, managing to get lost in the naval yard complex after getting dropped off around the corner!

Thursday 11th October 2007

Our last full day in Boston before flying back home, and although we should have made more of it and get up early to do some proper sightseeing, that was never likely to happen given the late night we'd had. I was still up at a reasonable time though and had a good swim in the pool (nothing to do with escaping the snoring!), but once we finally left the hotel it was gone midday, so we got a taxi to the Elephant & Castle for some brunch, a tasty shepherd's pie. The place was busy with office workers but soon emptied once they returned to their offices, and we decided to walk around and look in the shops for souvenirs and presents.

The obvious place to head for souvenir shops was the Quincy Market, which is the most visited tourist destination in Boston and has its origins in pre-independence days, consisting of a large Georgian style building with small shops and stalls, inside and outside, at ground level and at basement level. We spent a fair bit of time there, being mindful of the fact that we were limited with what could be carried back in our rucksacks, but ended up with a combination of calendars, hot pepper sauces (including one called "the hottest f****** sauce in the world", which turned out to be much hotter than your average supermarket hot pepper sauce, but I subsequently had even hotter ones from a website called chilliworld.com), sweets and other souvenirs and presents. Once we'd finished shopping we had a beer at the Cheers Bar (not the one featured in the TV series, but the one at Quincy Market), and then got a taxi back to the hotel so we could dump our shopping off before heading out for the last night of the trip.

Having been to the Hard Rock Café in New York (and I'd been to the one in Niagara Falls, New York, previously), we decided to start the night off with a visit to the Boston Hard Rock Café, so got a taxi from the hotel. All previous taxi drivers in New York and Boston had been of foreign origin with little apparent command of English and little attempt to communicate other than establishing the destination and fare. This one on the other hand was Boston born and bred and was a right laugh! Non-stop banter all the way into town. I said to him "it's good to have a driver who speaks English", and he replied "is that what they tell ya, they're full of cr*p, they have to speak English to get their f*****g licence, but they pretend to the tourists they can't speak much English cos they're so f*****g miserable. 'Hey I'm looking for the Radisson, you know the one that was on that three hour f*****g exam you took', 'Oh yes, I know the Radisson', 'well f*****g right you do'. I should go and work in Haiti and say 'hey dude I don't speak Creole', what the f**k………". Kept us amused all the way to the Hard Rock Café, except he took us to the old location having forgotten it had moved locations, so took us to the new location for the same price. We weren't complaining, a few more minutes entertainment from the driver / stand up comedian!

As with the visit to the Hard Rock Café at Times Square, we sat at the bar, enjoying a few beers and talking about all sorts, reflecting on the previous three weeks of travelling from the Pacific to Atlantic coasts of North America. The Hard Rock Café is on Clinton Street, just across the road from where we'd been drinking the night before, so after there we walked up Union Street into a bar called the Union Oyster Bar, which was fairly quiet but a decent place. We couldn't help laughing at a poster on the wall though. No idea what it was for, just one of those painted posters that you see in pubs, saying "you're in good hands", and had two men pictured on it. The thing is, one looked exactly like Paul Whitehouse from 'The Fast Show' (classic BBC comedy from the 1990s), and the other looked exactly like Ronnie Barker from his 'Open All Hours' days! Seemed funny at the time anyway and was worthy of a photo.

From there we went to The Point, where we'd been the night before, although were disappointed to find that the juke box was off due a band setting up. Seemed like a small space to have a band playing, and I hate having my ear drums blasted by music in small places like that, so we didn't stay there long. We walked along Hanover Street in the search of another bar, found that it was mostly cafes and restaurants along there, but it began to absolutely pour down so we went into the Café Paradise for a drink and to escape the rain. With the apparent lack of bars along there, we got a taxi down to Cornwalls where we'd had lunch the day before.

Cornwalls is one of those pubs that has a selection of board games on offer to help keep customers entertained, so we couldn't resist a game of Battleships, something neither of us had played in 15-20 years! With the fine selection of whiskies in there I decided to have a Glenlivet single malt, which is one of the distilleries I've been to but unfortunately when I was only about 12! Whisky isn't something I can drink fast or much of though, I prefer to take my time and enjoy it, so the rounds got out of synch somewhat, but to finish the night off Dan got some sambucas in, which went down a treat. Before getting a taxi back to the hotel, we went into the shop across the road to get some munchies, and with Dan now in his 'talk to anyone' mood he had great fun talking to a 'bag lady' type character who was trying to decide between buying spaghetti or meatballs for her dinner. Funny, but one of those where you had to be there! Once back at the hotel, we polished off the rum, ate the food we'd bought at the shop, and that was that, the last night in Boston, the last night of the trip, all ready for the flight home the next day.

Chapter 6 – Homeward Bound

Friday 12th October 2007

With the flight not being until 7-10pm we had a long day of waiting around ahead of us, and after checking out of the hotel at 11am we got a taxi to the Elephant & Castle for some brunch. I went for bangers & mash but no beer, opting for some tea instead. The office workers filled the place around midday, and after a couple of hours in there we decided to get a taxi up to the airport, as we didn't fancy a session in the pub or walking around with our bags. Once checked in we went through security, which seemed to take ridiculously long and got a bit frustrating, then we sat around and had a few drinks as we waited in the departure lounge. I opted for some red wine to hopefully help me sleep on the plane, but only a couple of glasses. I usually find when on holiday and sat waiting for the flight home it's the time when I just want to be magically transported back home in an instant, rather than sit around in airports and spend a night on a plane. Still, it was quite good to be sat there reflecting on the previous three weeks of adventure.

The only disappointing thing about the flight was that because it was KLMs partner airline, North West Airlines, that operated the flight, they opened up the online check in to their own customers first, so we had a limited choice of seats to choose from. We still got a couple of seats together so not too bad, just not the preferred back of the plane seats like we had to Vancouver. The flight itself took off a few minutes early, and once the meals had been served, eaten and cleared, I managed to get about an hours sleep, before deciding I couldn't sleep anymore so changed my watch to Amsterdam time.

Saturday 13th October 2007

It was daylight as we came down over the UK so got some fine views there, then across the North Sea to Amsterdam, where we arrived 20 minutes ahead of our ETA of 8am. Having said that, the size of Schiphol Airport means that taxiing to the gate seems to take forever, so we actually got off the plane pretty much on time. We both had just over an hour until our respective flights, and our luggage was transferred automatically to the next planes, so we had time for a quick coffee at the bar we'd had lunch at 3 weeks previously, then went our separate ways.

At the departure gate for the flight to Teesside I recognised someone from watching Darlington matches, couldn't actually remember his name (Andy) until later but got talking to him, and as he ended up being sat in the row in front of me I talked to him for much of the short flight back across the North Sea. It really did seem like a short flight, hardly even a flight at all, after the long trans-Atlantic flight from Boston I'd just been on. After an hour we were back on English soil, I was reunited with my rucksack, my dad picked me up in my car and I was back home for 10am. Lots of proper tea, Sky Sports News, looked at the photos of the trip on the laptop, England 3 Estonia 0 in the football, England 14 France 9 in the rugby World Cup semi-final, and finally a good 12 hour sleep in my own bed, with no one's snoring to keep me awake! Home sweet home after another amazing trans-North American rail journey.

It had been an amazing three weeks of travel, enjoying both the experience of seeing things again and the experience of seeing new things. It was great to go back to Vancouver, revisit some of the bars and shops seen last time, but great to see so much more of the city this time, going across to North Vancouver and the Capilano bridge, doing the bus tour, and having far better weather (except when in cloud up Grouse Mountain!). It was great to go back to Jasper and stay in the same hotel, but great to go up Whistlers Mountain, have a go at driving, and visit the Athabasca glacier. It was great to visit Toronto for the third time, staying at the same hotel as last time and going to some of the same bars, but great to see more of the city by doing the bus tour, see some football, and visit more bars. It was great to visit New York again and see the sights, but great to see more with the bus tours, Staten Island ferry, and stay in a better hotel than previously. As for Boston, like the train journey south of the border to New York, that was all new to me and a great experience.

On the second trip I'd had the bonus of a digital camera, so took far more pictures than on the first trip, many of which have been printed, framed, and now hang on my walls at home, including a special six picture 'Jasper galley' in my living room. Of all the places I think Jasper is where I'd like to go back to most, it really is one of my favourite places in the world. Three week holidays in North America are quite expensive though, so not sure when I'll do another one, but I definitely plan on doing another coast to coast trip some day, probably Halifax to Quebec City to Toronto to Winnipeg to Edmonton to Jasper to Vancouver.

In the meantime, in April 2009 me and Dan returned to Toronto with a couple of friends, Chris (the one who'd sent me score updates of England v Azerbaijan when I was on the train through Nova Scotia, and who phoned me when I was at the hockey in Winnipeg), and Adam, another Darlo fan, where we had 4 nights before taking the train to New York for a further 4 nights. We flew KLM again via Amsterdam, stayed in the Days Inn on Carlton Street again in Toronto, stayed in the Pod Hotel in New York again, but this time we travelled first class for the train to New York, only another £25 and much better seats with free non-alcoholic drinks for the whole journey, well worth it. We had a day where we saw both Toronto FC and Toronto Maple Leafs lose (the latter to the Montreal

Canadiens, which made me feel nearly as gutted as when Darlington got beat 3-0 at home to Hartlepool in 2007!), visited a greater variety of bars as well as old favourites, and I had my 4th visit to the CN Tower in Toronto and 2nd to the Empire State Building in New York.

This time in New York though we took a 3 hour boat trip around the island of Manhattan which was fantastic, got the Staten Island ferry again but this time went for a beer (felt very eerie as I looked at where I'd been sat at the ferry terminal 18 months previously when I got the message about my aunt), and we took the Subway to a random stop in the Bronx, which was an experience! All in all a fantastic trip to build on the previous visits, and to build on what I've said above about the joys of revisiting places yet seeing new things in those places. I also managed to see the Leafs win 4-1 in New Jersey, at their new arena in Newark, which helped to make up for the disappointment of losing 6-2 to Montreal, although I'd have happily swapped the scores around.

Another highlight of the 2009 trip was a coach trip to the Niagara Falls with Gray Line Tours. This included a delicious buffet lunch at the 5 star Sheraton Hotel at Niagara Falls, a trip to the falls, and wine tasting at the Pillitteri winery near Niagara on the Lake, where they make ice wine – a very sweet dessert wine made with grapes harvested in January at sub zero temperatures. We even had time for a beer in the Hard Rock Cafe in Niagara Falls, so I've now been to one on either side of the border there! The only downside was the stubborn low cloud which refused to leave the area where the falls are, so we couldn't really see anything of the falls until we were 20 feet away, although it was good to go in the tunnels underneath which I hadn't done before. The driver Patrick was also a good laugh, always talking and kept us informed of the sights, and very appreciative of the $10 tip we each gave him.

Although more of a country person than a city person, Toronto and New York are two great cities with so much to see and do, and I'm sure I'll be going back in the not too distant future, especially with my love of the Toronto Maple Leafs! It's also good to see other people enjoying first hand what you've told them about from previous visits, and later recalling their own highlights and memories to add to one's own perspective – my brother experiencing Vancouver, Jasper, Toronto and New York for the first time in 2007 after hearing about my trips of 2005 and 2006, and Chris and Adam experiencing Toronto and New York for the first time in 2009, where we retraced part of our 2007 journey and my other visits to those cities.

Looking back at these trips across 'the pond', I think it's only fair to nominate some awards. So, in no particular order: my favourite beer? Alexander Keith's India Pale Ale, Canada's finest. Best hotel? Whistlers

Inn at Jasper, especially in 2007, although the Listel in Vancouver isn't far behind. Best food? L&Ws in Jasper, all of the meals were superb, although the Five Fishermen in Halifax isn't far behind. Best view? Top of Whistlers Mountain, Jasper. Best boat trip? Whale watching off Vancouver Island, the exhilaration just about beats the sightseeing of Manhattan, and the paddling at Pyramid Lake! Best ice hockey team? Toronto Maple Leafs of course, who I've seen win three times but lose twice! Best museum? Historic Fort York, Toronto. Best tall building? CN Tower, amazing views and not much queuing. Best helicopter ride? Manhattan, unbeatable. Best flight? The float plane from Vancouver to Victoria, great experience. Best bus tour? Niagara Falls, although the city tours in Vancouver, Toronto and New York were all brilliant. Best place for people watching? Times Square, New York, from an open top bus on a sunny day. Best food tried for first time? Halibut in Vancouver, although elk burger in Jasper and bison hot pot in Winnipeg were both memorable. Most photographed landmark? CN Tower, must be on every other photo from the 2006 visit to Toronto! Most visited bar? Hoops at Yonge Street, Toronto. Funny how I've started and finished these awards with beer related topics!

So there we have it, my story of two epic trips across North America, with two shorter trips thrown in to build on the previous visits. It's been a real pleasure recalling such great memories. It's been an adventure in itself writing this book which I began before setting off on the first trip in 2005. I hope it's been a pleasure reading about all the travelling, and I hope it's inspired you to visit wherever it is you want to go in the world, especially if it's Canada or the USA, places I'll always go back to. I've certainly enhanced my life experience by travelling across Canada and the USA on the trips I've described, and that's what's it's all about, enjoying life. Now get out there and enjoy it!

Printed in Great Britain
by Amazon.co.uk, Ltd.,
Marston Gate.